The Encyclopedia of the
Summer Olympics

The Encyclopedia of the
Summer Olympics

Written by David Fischer

FRANKLIN WATTS
A Division of Scholastic Inc.

New York • Toronto • London • Auckland • Sydney
Mexico City • New Delhi • Hong Kong
Danbury, Connecticut

Developed for Franklin Watts by Visual Education Corporation, Princeton, New Jersey

For Visual Education
Project Director: Jewel G. Moulthrop
Associate Editor: Cheryl MacKenzie
Copyediting: Helen A. Castro
Photo Research: Sara Matthews, Ben Bryer, Chad Saharic
Production Supervisor: Sara Matthews
Cover Design: Maxson Crandall
Interior Design: John Romer
Electronic Preparation: Fiona Torphy
Electronic Production: Rob Ehlers, Lisa Evans-Skopas, Laura Watson-Sarnoski

The editorial materials presented in this publication are the sole responsibility of Franklin Watts, a Division of Scholastic Inc.

Library of Congress Cataloging-in-Publication Data
Fischer, David, 1963-
   The encyclopedia of the Summer Olympics/David Fischer.
      p.   cm. — (Watts reference)
   Summary: Explores the history and traditions of the Olympics and
   the various events included in the competitions held every four years.
   Includes bibliographical references and index.
      ISBN 0-531-11886-X (lib. bdg.)   0-531-16392-X (pbk.)
1. Olympics—Encyclopedias—Juvenile literature. [1. Olympics.]
I. Title. II. Series.
GV721.5 .F54   2003
796.48—dc21
                                                    2002038024

Printed in the United States

1 2 3 4 5 6 7 8 9 10 R 12 11 10 09 08 07 06 05 04 03

TABLE OF CONTENTS

Note: In this book you will find separate articles about the athletes whose names appear in SMALL CAPITAL LETTERS. Check the Table of Contents for the appropriate page numbers.

OLYMPIC HISTORY

According to legend, the Olympic Games commemorated the victory of Zeus, ruler of all the Greek gods. Zeus had defeated his father, Kronos, in a battle on Mount Olympus for control of the world. The first recorded games occurred in Olympia in 776 B.C.—more than 2,700 years ago. The champion of that competition was Coroebus, who won a footrace of about 200 yards (183 meters). He was crowned with branches from a sacred olive tree believed to have been planted by Hercules at the Temple of Zeus. Thereafter, Olympic festivals were held every four years.

During a time when wars between city-states were almost constant, the games imposed a period of truce. Wars ceased and trade between cities stopped. Travelers to and from the festival were granted safe passage, and all weapons were barred from Olympia for the duration of the games. Nothing interfered with the competition.

This Greek vase, dating from around the 500s B.C., depicts a four-horse chariot race, an event in the ancient Olympics.

The ancient Olympics were spiritual gatherings. After taking an oath of purity and pledging to honor the gods, athletes underwent a rigorous ten-month training period under the supervision of special judges called *Hellanodikai.* The best athletes in each sport were chosen to compete in running, jumping, and throwing events. The strongest became wrestlers or boxers. These games were also bloody affairs. In the *pankration*—a battle to the death—two contestants fought until only one remained standing.

At first, officials barred women from either participating in the activities or even watching them. The competition was strictly for men, who performed in the nude. Contestants came from all social classes, including slaves. Many were men of means who could afford to take more than ten months away from their regular duties to train and compete. Others were fortunate enough to have a wealthy patron to sponsor them. While in training, athletes were provided with food and clothing. Winners at the games received ample rewards of money, property, and gifts. The ancient Olympics were awe-inspiring religious events, and the status of athletes reached godlike proportions. The athlete's struggle was romanticized in poetry and his artistic form depicted on vases. The very best were immortalized as statues.

When Rome conquered Greece in 146 B.C., the games lost their religious significance. In A.D. 393, the Roman emperor Theodosius I, a Christian, declared the Olympics a pagan ritual and abolished them. He then ordered the destruction of all statues of Greek gods. The Olympics disappeared for more than 1,500 years.

The Olympic Revival

The modern Olympics owe their existence to the efforts of one man: Baron Pierre de Coubertin. Born in France in 1863, Coubertin had a lifelong passion for sports and grew up to be an educator in the French Sports Ministry. He strongly believed that amateur sports have a positive influence on society. When German archaeologist Ernst Curtius uncovered the stadium ruins at Olympia in the 1870s, Coubertin visited the site and was inspired by the ancient Greek tradition. He decided that a revival of the Olympic Games would restore pride among nations and promote world peace.

Although his idea was greeted with skepticism, the wealthy Frenchman persisted. In 1894, Coubertin met with amateur sports representatives from nine nations, including the United States and Russia, to outline his Olympic vision. Coubertin delivered a stirring speech at the meeting. He said that while hopes to completely eliminate war were foolish, hopes to reduce the chance of war were not: "The telegraph, railroads, and telephone have done more for peace than all the treaties and diplomatic conventions. I expect that athleticism will do even more."

The baron's passionate words won the support of the delegates, who voted unanimously to organize the first modern games in 1896. Appropriately, they selected Athens, Greece, as the site for the games. The Olympics received no financial support from the government of Greece. A private organizing committee raised funds for the event by selling souvenir stamps and medals.

Founder of the modern Olympic Games, Baron Pierre de Coubertin was passionate about sports and believed that the games would promote world peace.

Spyridon Louis, in his traditional dress, poses with athletes and officials at the first modern Olympiad.

The First Modern Olympiad

On April 6, 1896, King George I of Greece declared the first modern Olympic Games open. Thirteen nations sent 311 athletes, all of them men, to Athens to compete in nine sports including track and field, fencing, and swimming. A German gymnast named Hermann Weingartner won three events and became the most decorated athlete in Athens. Winners were awarded a diploma and a silver medal because gold was considered too expensive.

The Greeks fared better than any other nation, yet only one event really mattered to them: the marathon, a 26-mile (42-kilometer) race. A shepherd named Spyridon Louis gave the Greeks their first track-and-field victory on the final day of the games. As Louis headed into the Olympic stadium in Athens, two Greek princes left their seats and jumped onto the track to run alongside him as he reached the finish line.

The success of the games inspired Coubertin to compose the Olympic oath. This oath is still recited at the opening ceremonies by athletes who pledge to participate "in the true spirit of sportsmanship." Coubertin served as the first president of the International Olympic Committee (IOC), a position he held until 1924. His greatest legacy—the Olympic flag—is one of the most recognized symbols in the world. Its five interlocking circles represent the five major continents: Europe, Asia, Africa, the Americas, and Australia. The

THE INTERCALATED GAMES

After the disappointing turnout at the 1900 and 1904 games, Greece staged the Intercalated Games of 1906. (The word *intercalate* means "to insert in the calendar.") This competition, although not considered official by the International Olympic Committee, nevertheless kept up the Olympic spirit until the next official Olympics in 1908.

colors of the rings are always the same, from left to right: blue, yellow, black, green, and red. At least one of these colors appears on every flag of every nation in the world.

Off to a Slow Start

Coubertin urged that the 1900 Olympic Games coincide with the Paris International Exposition of art and industry. He reasoned that the attention already given to this world fair would help increase enthusiasm for the games. His plan backfired, however, because the fair upstaged the competition. In addition, the soccer and water polo tournaments took over five months to complete, and spectators lost interest.

The IOC initially awarded the 1904 games to the city of Chicago. President Theodore Roosevelt, however, ordered that the games be relocated to St. Louis as part of the World's Fair. As had happened in 1900, the fair overshadowed the Olympics. Coubertin did not even bother to attend. Very few foreign athletes traveled to these games. American athletes, who often found themselves competing against their own teammates, won 214 medals. This Olympiad was the first at which gold, silver, and bronze medals were awarded for first, second, and third place, respectively.

The opening ceremony at the 1908 games in London, England, began as the athletes marched into the stadium nation by nation, each team walking behind its country's flag. Diving and field hockey made their debut, as did figure skating, which was moved to the Winter Olympics when they began in 1924. The British team won an astonishing 146 medals, causing skeptical American officials to complain that British judges had shown favoritism to the hometown athletes. As a result, the IOC decided to use judges from several different countries at future games.

The Games Grow Up

Athletes representing all five major continents met for the first time at the 1912 Olympiad. Nearly 2,500 athletes from 28 countries were represented in Stockholm, Sweden. The outbreak of World War I (1914–1918) caused the cancellation of the 1916 Olympic Games. When the games resumed in 1920 in Antwerp, Belgium, the nations that had been defeated in the war—Germany, Austria, Hungary, Bulgaria, and Turkey—were not invited. The Olympic flag made its first appearance that year and quickly became a part of the opening ceremonies. In each Olympiad since then, the flag has been handed over to the mayor of the host city by the mayor of the previous host city. It is then raised as the Olympic song plays in the background. Once the games and closing ceremonies have concluded, the flag is kept in the host city's town hall until the next competition.

The last Olympiad that Coubertin organized was held in 1924 in Paris, France. Earlier that same year, the first Winter Games had taken place. Coubertin had seen his dream fulfilled. He had witnessed the personification of the Olympic motto: *Citius, Altius, Fortius.* These words are Latin for "Faster, Higher, Stronger." They describe what Olympic athletes strive for: to be the best.

An atmosphere of international harmony marked the 1928 games in Amsterdam, Holland, after World War I. Gold medals were spread among more nations (28) than ever before. The number of women athletes doubled to 290 because they were now allowed to compete in track-and-field events. When several female runners collapsed in exhaustion after the 800-meter race, however, the IOC banned all women's races longer than 200 meters (219 yards). Until 1960, no women's race could be longer than one-half lap around the Olympic track, which is 400 m (438 yds) long.

The 1932 Summer Games were held during the Great Depression in Los Angeles, California. Only 1,328 athletes took part—the lowest turnout since 1904. American athletes won 103 medals, more than any other nation. Americans also broke or tied many of the 18 world records during the 16 days of competition. The crowds set records as well. One million people paid to attend these games, which were the first Summer Olympics to turn a profit.

Controversy Taints the Games

Intolerance threatened the 1936 games even before they began. Planning for the competition began in 1931, when the IOC chose Berlin to host the 11th modern Olympiad. No

Adolf Hitler used the 1936 games in Berlin to promote the German idea of a master race. His racist beliefs, however, were disproved when African-American athlete Jesse Owens won four gold medals.

objections were raised until Adolf Hitler and the Nazi Party came to power in Germany two years later. The Nazis believed in the superiority of the "Aryan" race and discriminated against certain groups of people in Germany, especially Jews. Concerned that Hitler would use the Olympics to encourage racial discrimination and anti-Semitism, the IOC considered—but ultimately decided against—moving the games elsewhere.

The 1936 competition went off as scheduled, and Hitler did indeed manipulate the pageantry of the Olympic traditions. During the opening ceremony, uniformed German soldiers marched in the Parade of Nations with arms raised in the Nazi salute. Their victory call *"Sieg Heil!"* sounded over the loudspeakers. Huge banners displaying the Nazi swastika, or cross, were flown alongside the Olympic flag as the torchbearer arrived in the stadium to light the Olympic flame. It was a disturbing mix of Olympic and military symbolism.

Although Germany set the winning standard with 33 gold medals, the success of African-American athletes—particularly JESSE OWENS—destroyed Hitler's myth of white supremacy. This was not the last time that the Olympics would be influenced by politics, nor the last time that the games would rise above it.

Politics and the Olympic Games

World War II (1939–1945) prevented the next two Summer Olympiads, scheduled for 1940 and 1944, from taking place. The IOC selected London, England, to host the 1948 games. Although the Soviet Union had joined the IOC the previous year, Soviet sports officials decided not to send an official team to London. Instead they prepared for 1952, when the games would be played across the Russian border in Helsinki, Finland.

The Soviets took an early lead at the 1952 games when their women gymnasts won the overall competition, starting a trend that would last for the next 40 years. The United States responded with stunning victories in swimming, diving, boxing, and weightlifting to push ahead in the final medal count, 76–71. Thus began a medals race between the superpowers that would last for decades.

The Soviet drive for medals resumed in 1956. For the first time, the games were held in the Southern Hemisphere—in Melbourne, Australia. Not long before the opening ceremony, Russian tanks rolled into Budapest to crush the Hungarian Revolution. The bitter feelings between the Hungarians and the Soviets carried over into the Olympics. Hostilities erupted during the water polo match between the two countries. The clash became a ferocious fistfight, and the match was halted. The rivalries between athletes from the United States and the Soviet Union turned into a duel between the ideologies of capitalism and communism. The Russians made a convincing argument for athletic achievement under communism by winning 98 medals. America and the rest of the free world struggled to keep pace.

Although the Soviet team dominated many sports, especially the women's events, it was not until the 1960 Summer Olympics that the Soviets began to challenge the U.S. men's track-and-field team as well. The games in Rome that year hinted that a profound "changing of the guard" was occurring. For the first time since the beginning of the modern games, Eastern-bloc nations won several sprinting events, which had previously been locked up by English-speaking countries.

More than 5,000 athletes from 93 nations descended on Tokyo in 1964 as the Summer Olympics came to Asia for the first time. Japan, ready to assume its place in the world after a devastating defeat in World War II, saw the games as an opportunity to rebuild the cities that had been destroyed by the atomic bomb. A young Japanese man, born in 1945 near Hiroshima just hours after the world's first nuclear explosion, carried the Olympic torch into the stadium to begin the games.

South Africa was banned from competition because of its government's segregationist policies, called apartheid, which deprived black South Africans of their civil rights. The ban was lifted in time for the 1992 games, after a change of government in South Africa ended apartheid.

As part of the Soviet team, gymnast Larysa Latynina won a total of 18 medals between 1956 and 1964, more than any other athlete in Olympic history.

IOC Gets Tough

Throughout Olympic history, the games have been a reflection of society. The 1960s were an emotionally charged decade. The struggle over human rights and the Vietnam War, in particular, resulted in assassination attempts, civil rights protests, and antiwar rallies. At the 1968 Summer Olympics in Mexico City, the spirit of the decade finally invaded the Olympic movement.

These games were rocked by protests over racial injustice. Sprinters Tommie Smith and John Carlos caused a sensation on the victory platform after the 200-meter dash by bowing their heads and raising gloved fists in the air during the playing of the U.S. national anthem. They intended this public protest to increase awareness of the prejudicial treatment of African-Americans in sports and society. Angered by this dramatic yet nonviolent protest, IOC president Avery Brundage expelled both athletes from the Olympic Village.

At first it seemed that the 1972 Summer Olympics in Munich would be remembered for the athletic history created when MARK SPITZ won seven gold medals, all in world-record times. Then, on September 5, a horrifying event occurred. Palestinian terrorists, armed with machine guns, made their way into the Olympic Village, murdered two members of the Israeli team, and took another nine Israelis hostage. An image of the terrorists in ski masks was broadcast on live television throughout the world. The nine hostages and the terrorists died later during a daring attempt by police to rescue the hostages. As the Olympic flag stood at half-mast, a memorial service was held for the murdered Israelis. The IOC debated whether to end the competition but decided to continue the games.

Raising their gloved fists and bowing their heads, Tommie Smith and John Carlos sent a message to the world about racism.

Olympics Surrender to Boycotts

The Olympic spirit is resilient, and athletes recovered from the Munich attack. But the Olympic movement had already been affected by politics long before the games came to Moscow in 1980. When the Soviet Union invaded Afghanistan that year, U.S. president

German police attempt to rescue nine Israelis held hostage by Palestinian terrorists in the Olympic Village during the 1972 games in Munich.

Jimmy Carter called for a boycott of the Moscow games. The United States and 60 other countries stayed home. Hundreds of athletes lost their chance to compete for an Olympic medal. In an act of revenge four years later, the Soviet Union and other Eastern-bloc nations boycotted the Los Angeles games. American athletes, competing against few real rivals, won 83 gold medals.

After the two boycotts, the Olympic movement was floundering. Cities had lost interest in hosting the games. Luckily the Los Angeles games reversed this trend and demonstrated how sports could tap into big business and enjoy the economic boom of the 1980s. The 1984 games were the first since 1896 to be staged without government financing. The Los Angeles organizers arranged for large companies to become official sponsors of the games. This innovative strategy produced a $250 million profit and launched an era of widespread corporate involvement.

Changes: Good and Bad

With so much money available, the Olympics were growing out of control. Even athletes were amazed at the monetary rewards, such as product endorsements they could claim by winning a medal. Some began to use performance-enhancing drugs, such as anabolic steroids, to gain an edge over their opponents. Although relatively few athletes had tested positive for drugs since 1972, when the IOC instituted drug testing, the issue erupted at the 1988 games in Seoul, South Korea. That year, Canadian sprinter Ben Johnson set a world record in the 100-meter dash. He then tested positive for steroids and was stripped of his gold medal in disgrace.

Following the 1988 Olympics, the world experienced massive political changes. Much of the turmoil that had resulted in boycotts between 1976 and 1988 evaporated as many of the communist nations gained their independence from the Soviet Union. In 1989, the Berlin Wall came down, and athletes from West Germany and East Germany formed a single, awe-inspiring team. The Unified Team of former Soviet republics competed for the first and only time at the 1992 Olympics in Barcelona, Spain.

There were other changes as well. Although the qualifications for amateur status were very strict, some countries had bent the rules in order to allow professionals to compete. The new IOC president, Juan Antonio Samaranch, believed that Olympic events should be competitions among the world's best athletes, so he changed the long-standing policy that barred professional athletes from the games.

The U.S. Dream Team dominated the basketball competition of the 1992 games, the first time the IOC allowed professional athletes to participate in the games.

Following the 1988 games, the IOC voted to allow professional athletes to compete in the Olympics. Professional basketball players competed at the Barcelona games. The United States recruited 12 of the greatest National Basketball Association (NBA) players in the world to play together on the so-called Dream Team. As expected, the team that included Michael Jordan, Magic Johnson, and Patrick Ewing easily won the gold medal. They created an odd image on the victory platform because some athletes covered their team logo with that of the company whose products they endorsed.

The 1996 games in Atlanta, Georgia, were extra special because this Olympiad was the 100th anniversary of the modern games. In many ways the Olympics had never been bigger or better. A record 10,310 athletes from 197 nations competed in 271 events. The viewing audience was dismayed by the commercialism that surrounded the competition, however. On the eighth day of the games, tragedy struck the Olympics once again. A bomb exploded in Centennial Olympic Park, killing one person and injuring 110 others. The crime remains unsolved.

Against a backdrop of bribes paid to IOC members and the time zone difference that resulted in tape-delayed television coverage, the 2000 Summer Olympics in Sydney, Australia, failed to capture the attention of fans. For Australians, the moment to remember was when runner Cathy Freeman won the women's 400-meter race and the first-ever victory for an Aborigine, the native black culture of Australia. Freeman took a victory lap with both the Australian and the Aboriginal flags draped over her shoulder.

Future Games

Athens, Greece, will host the Summer Olympic Games in August 2004. The Athens games are expected to be the largest Summer Games ever, with 11,000 athletes and officials from nearly 200 countries. Television networks have paid staggering fees for the rights to broadcast the games worldwide. An estimated 3 billion viewers will watch more than 170 hours on live television. The games have truly become a major global extravaganza and are expected to remain so.

PASSING THE TORCH

One year before Baron Pierre de Coubertin's death in 1937, a German member of the International Olympic Committee revived the idea of an Olympic flame that burned for the duration of the games. The concept derives from the ancient Greeks, who used a flame lit by the sun's rays at Olympia, the site of the original games. Today, leading up to the opening ceremonies, a series of runners relays the Olympic torch into the stadium. The last runner circles the track in the stadium before igniting the Olympic flame. Symbolizing the spirit of peaceful competition, doves are released after the lighting of the flame.

ARCHERY

Archery is the sport of shooting at targets with a bow and arrow. A successful archer requires steady hands, strong arms, and sharp eyes.

Origin of the Sport

Prehistoric people invented the bow and arrow thousands of years ago as a weapon for hunting and war. Over the centuries, many advances in archery have been made. Archery developed as a sport in England in the 1500s. During the reign of King Henry VIII, from 1509 to 1547, all men under the age of 60 were required to practice shooting with a longbow, and archery contests became popular events during festivals. After firearms replaced the bow and arrow as England's chief weapons of war in the 1600s, archery was practiced more exclusively as a sport.

Archery became an official Olympic event at the 1900 games in Paris, France. It was also featured at the games in 1904, 1908, and 1920. Due to a lack of interest and no internationally accepted rules, archery was dropped from the Olympic program. In 1931, an international governing body for archery was founded. Called the Federation Internationale de Tir a l'Arc (FITA), the organization established a system of rules for competitions. Because of FITA's enthusiastic promotion of the sport, archery reappeared as an official Olympic event at the 1972 games in Munich, Germany, and has remained an Olympic sport.

Competing in the Event

Archers attempt to score the most points by hitting the smallest inner ring, or bull's-eye, on the circular target. The target, which is 48 inches (122 centimeters) in diameter, has 10 rings. A hit in the outermost ring is worth only one point. The rings increase in value by one point as they near the bull's-eye, which is worth 10 points. An archer scores a "Robin Hood" when he or she shoots an arrow into the shaft of an arrow already in the bull's-eye. This feat is equivalent to a hole-in-one in golf.

Fast Facts

First Olympic competition

London, England; 1908

Legendary athletes

Kim Soo Nyung,
South Korea

Criteria for winning

Highest score

Olympic archers use the recurve bow, which features tips that curve away from the archer. The bow is typically made of wood covered in fiberglass or graphite. Most bowstrings are manufactured from a hydrocarbon, although some are made of Kevlar, the material used to make bulletproof vests. The arrows, which can reach speeds of over 150 miles (241 kilometers) per hour, are usually made of aluminum or carbon graphite.

In addition to a bow and arrow, archers require safety equipment. Arm guards protect the forearm of the hand that holds the bow when the bowstring snaps back after it is released. Many archers also wear a shooting glove to protect the fingers that draw the bowstring.

Archers require great strength. The average bow has a draw weight of 50 pounds (23 kilograms). The draw weight is the number of pounds required to pull back the bowstring. Archers also need excellent vision and aim. At 229 feet and 8 inches (70 meters) away, the target looks about the size of a thumbtack held at arm's length.

There are four archery events held at the Olympics: men's individual, women's individual, men's team, and women's team. Team competitions are similar to individual competitions. Each team is composed of three archers. Each

Surprise winner Justin Huish was ranked 24th in the world when he upset the top contender in the individual archery competition in 1996.

WHEELCHAIR ARCHERS

In 1984, Neroli Fairhall of New Zealand made Olympic archery history. Paralyzed from the waist down, Fairhall shot her arrows from a wheelchair, placing 35th. In 1996, Italy's Paola Fantato became the second archer to compete from a wheelchair. He placed 54th.

At the opening ceremony of the 1992 Olympics in Barcelona, Spain, paralympics archer Antonio Rebollo of Spain lit the Olympic flame by shooting a fiery arrow into the air, igniting the flame.

competition begins with a ranking round during which each archer shoots a total of 72 arrows at the target. In individual competition, the top 64 archers in the ranking round advance to the elimination round. During the elimination round, each archer shoots 18 arrows at the target with a 40-second time limit for each shot. Eight winners then move on to the semifinal and final rounds.

In the semifinal and final rounds, each archer shoots a total of 12 arrows with the same time limit as during the elimination round. Archers who do not qualify for the finals compete for the bronze medal, while the winning semifinalists vie for the gold and silver medals.

The rules are the same for men and women. In the individual competition, the 64 best archers shoot in pairs. The winners advance, and the losers are eliminated. Archers shoot 18 arrows in each of the first three rounds, and 12 arrows in each of the final three rounds. In the first three rounds, archers shoot from four distances: 90, 70, 50, and 30 m (approximately 98, 77, 55, and 33 yds, respectively). In the final two rounds, those distances are reversed.

In the Olympics

Hubert van Innis of Belgium is probably the most successful archer in Olympic history. His performances during the 1900 and 1920 games earned him six gold and three silver medals. In 1996, Justin Huish of the United States caused a stir at the games in Atlanta, Georgia. Distinguished by his ponytail and the baseball cap he wore backwards, Huish won the gold after defeating the favored Michele Frangilli of Italy. He then helped the United States capture the gold for the first time in the men's team competition.

The women of South Korea have dominated the sport since 1972, winning more than ten gold medals, including the five individual titles and four team titles in a row. Kim Soo Nyung is one of the great female archers, with four Olympic gold medals, one silver, and one bronze to her name. In 2000, Kim Soo Nyung and her teammates, Yun Mi Jin and Kim Nam Soon, swept the individual medals and joined forces to easily capture South Korea's unprecedented fourth consecutive team championship.

BADMINTON

Badminton is one of the fastest racket sports in the world. Unlike other racket sports, which involve hitting a ball of some size, badminton players hit a shuttlecock, or birdie, and try to keep it from touching the ground.

Origin of the Sport

Sports similar to badminton were played in China over 2,000 years ago. One such game was *Ti Jian Zi,* or shuttlecock kicking. Players hit a shuttlecock with their hands or feet, or sometimes with a bat. In the 1300s in England, a game called battledore shuttlecock was played among the upper classes. Played without nets or boundaries, the game involved keeping the shuttlecock in play for as long as possible. In the late 1800s, the Duke of Beaufort, a great fan of the sport, introduced a net and boundaries to the game. The duke and his family frequently played the "new" game on their estate, called Badminton House, thus, the name *badminton.*

Soon afterward, British officers in India were playing badminton. They established a new set of rules, and badminton evolved into a competitive sport. By the beginning of the 20th century, the game had spread to Europe, Australia and New Zealand, and North America. From India, badminton spread throughout Asia, and by the late 1900s, Thailand, Indonesia, Japan, China, and Korea had risen to the top ranks of the sport.

Competing in the Event

In Olympic badminton, players use rackets that look like lightweight tennis rackets to whack a shuttlecock over a net. The net is 5 feet (1.5 meters) high and suspended off the ground. The court is 44 feet (13.4 m) long, divided into halves by the net.

The objective is to hit the birdie over the net and onto the opponent's side in a way that prevents the opponent from hitting it back. Badminton strategies are similar to those of tennis. Players try to catch opponents out of position by hitting long shots down the line and hard smashes over the net.

Fast Facts

First Olympic competition

Barcelona, Spain; 1992

Legendary athletes

Susi Susanti, **Indonesia**

Criteria for winning

Best two of three games

Susi Susanti of Indonesia won the women's gold medal at the 1992 games in Barcelona. This was the first Olympic gold medal ever won by an Indonesian athlete.

Good players play patiently, returning the shuttlecock again and again until the opponent makes a mistake or the player hits an unreturnable shot.

The shuttlecock, which weighs less than an ounce, has 14 to 16 goose feathers fixed in a cork base that is wrapped in leather or a similar material. When the shuttlecock is hit, air rushes over the feathers and squeezes them together. For an instant, the birdie is like a bullet piercing the air. In competitive play, shuttlecock speeds of 200 miles (320 kilometers) per hour have been recorded! Eventually the feathers open, returning the birdie to its parachute shape and slowing it down.

Players take turns serving, and only the serving player can score a point. If the server loses a rally, he loses his serve, but not the point. The server is allowed only one serve, which he must hit into the opposite service box. Both of the server's feet must be touching the court, and he must hit the birdie from below his waist with an underhand motion. The receiver cannot move before the serve is hit.

Men and women compete in singles, doubles, and mixed doubles. Games are played to 15 points, except for women's singles games, which are played to 11 points. A player or team must win two out of three games to win the match.

In the Olympics

Included in the Olympics as a demonstration sport in 1972 and an exhibition sport in 1988, badminton became a full medal sport in 1992. The best players are from Indonesia, Malaysia, China, South Korea, and Denmark, which has produced the only two non-Asian Olympic medalists.

In 1992, Indonesian players won five medals, ensuring the sport's popularity at home. Chinese women won five of the six medals at the 2000 games in Sydney, Australia. Chinese players Gu Jun and Ge Fei had been playing together since they were nine years old. Facing the reigning world champions—Korea's Gil Young-ah and Jang Hye-ock—the Chinese women attacked relentlessly and won the match and the gold in just 36 minutes.

BASEBALL

Although baseball is an American invention, the game is played and watched by millions of people in 120 countries. The object of the game is to score runs by advancing runners around three bases to home plate. When the player makes it safely around all the bases, he scores a point for his team. The team that scores the most runs by the end of nine innings wins.

Origin of the Sport

Baseball developed from an English game called rounders, in which players hit a pitched ball and run around posts (bases) to score a rounder (run). Baseball as it is played today began in Hoboken, New Jersey, in 1846. Alexander Cartwright, founder of the Knickerbocker Base Ball Club of New York, standardized the rules of the game. Cartwright's rules set the bases 90 feet apart, established a batting order in which players take turns hitting, and outlined the positions of the nine defensive players (pitcher, catcher, first baseman, second baseman, third baseman, shortstop, and three outfielders) on each team.

Soon after other ball clubs adopted the Knickerbocker rules, formal games became commonplace. The first organized baseball game was held in 1846 at the Elysian Fields in Hoboken. The Knickerbockers lost 23-1 to the New York Nine. Formal rules and organized games helped popularize the sport throughout the United States. Referred to as America's pastime for more than 140 years, baseball is one of the nation's first popular team games.

Baseball has been played in Europe since World War II, when American servicemen introduced the game in such countries as Italy and France. When Asian teams became consistent winners of the Little League World Series, Americans began to take notice of foreign competitors.

Competing in the Event

Baseball is played in nine innings, during which both teams have a turn at bat and a chance to score. The game is played with a bat, a ball, and a fielder's glove. Baseballs are made of

Fast Facts

First Olympic competition

Barcelona, Spain; 1992

Legendary athletes

Omar Linares, **Cuba**
Doug Mientkiewicz, **USA**

Criteria for winning

Most runs scored

SINGLE-HANDEDLY BRILLIANT

Jim Abbott is one of several Olympic baseball players who made it to the major leagues. Sheer determination to become a ball player compelled the young boy to spend hours throwing a ball against a brick wall. Eventually he perfected the moves that, from a distance, make it impossible to tell that Abbott has no right hand.

two pieces of cowhide stitched together over a ball of tightly wound string. At the center of the ball is a small, round cork coated with rubber. A baseball weighs 5 ounces (141.7 grams) and is 9 inches (22.8 centimeters) in circumference. Although the playing field is called a diamond, it is actually a slightly turned square with a base at each corner and an outfield.

The rules in Olympic baseball are basically the same as in the major leagues. A designated hitter may bat for the pitcher, and the use of aluminum bats is prohibited. The Olympic competition, however, has a so-called mercy rule. If a team is ahead by ten runs or more after seven innings, that team is declared the winner.

In the Olympics, teams compete in two divisions of four teams each. Each division plays a round robin, with the two top teams in each division advancing to the semifinal round. The first-place teams play the second-place teams in the other division. The winners of this round play for the gold medal; the losers play for the bronze.

In the Olympics

Baseball was included in the Summer Olympics as a demonstration sport six times before achieving official medal status in 1992. The Cuban team, with a record or 64 wins and 1 loss in international tournaments between 1986 and 1992, was the heavy favorite going into the Barcelona games. The Cubans swept through the tournament easily and took the gold. In nine games, they outscored their opponents 95 to 16. Their star player, third baseman Omar Linares, who has been called the best amateur baseball player in the world, batted .500 (meaning that he got a hit 50 percent of his turns at bat) and hit four home runs. Cuba repeated its victory in Atlanta four years later. Cuban players hit 38 home runs in 9 games, including 8 in the gold medal game alone and 8 by Linares.

The United States has never excelled in international baseball competition. Although the U.S. team won a medal in the demonstration game at the 1988 Olympics in Seoul, Korea, many believed it was only because Cuba had boycotted those games.

Cuba, the two-time defending gold medalist, was again favored to win at the 2000 Summer Olympics in Sydney, Australia. In a surprising upset, the Netherlands beat the Cubans 4-2, ending Cuba's remarkable 21-game Olympic winning streak. After defeating Korea, the U.S. team faced Cuba in the finals. The U.S. team jumped ahead immediately and set the tone with a first-inning home run by Mike Neill. Then the United States scored three runs in the fifth inning, sealing Cuba's fate. Ben Sheets, pitching for the United States, allowed only three hits and gave up zero runs to the Cubans. The Americans finished the game at four runs to zero.

The U.S. team made it to the final game thanks to Doug Mientkiewicz. In the semifinal round against South Korea, he hit a solo home run with one out in the bottom of the ninth inning to give the Americans a 3-2 victory and a chance at the gold. It was the second time in a week that Mientkiewicz had delivered the home run that won the game.

A Cuban player slides into base during a game against the United States at the Barcelona Olympiad. Cuba won the gold that year and returned in 1996 for a repeat Olympic victory.

BASKETBALL

In a regulation basketball game, two teams of five players each dribble and pass a ball down a court and score points by throwing it into the opponent's basket. The game's appeal, which crosses age, gender, class, and national lines, has attracted an estimated 200 million fans worldwide.

Origin of the Sport

In 1891, James Naismith, a Canadian student at a YMCA training college in Springfield, Massachusetts, was given the assignment to create a game that young men could play indoors. Naismith developed a basic set of rules and had the custodian nail two peach baskets to the railing at each end of the gymnasium. He then invited students and teachers to participate in the first basketball game. Played with a soccer ball and nine-man teams, that early game had no dribbling or free throws.

Over the years, basketball has undergone many rule changes. Free throws were introduced to the game in 1894. Dribbling was introduced by players at Yale University in 1896, but did not become part of the game until the 1930s. By that time, the game had become hugely popular. To add excitement to the play, officials eliminated the tip-off that followed every basket. Instead, the team that had been scored against took possession of the ball and threw it in from the end line beneath the basket.

The first professional basketball game was played in Trenton, New Jersey, in 1896. The early professional teams toured the country and challenged local teams to games and a share of the money from ticket sales. The Olympic organizing committee for the 1904 games in St. Louis included basketball as a demonstration sport. The game did not become a medal event until 1936.

In 1892, Senda Berenson, a gymnastics instructor at Smith College, introduced basketball to her female students. Within a year, the game was being played at several other prestigious women's colleges. Basketball has become a major sport for women. Women's basketball became an Olympic medal event in 1976.

Competing in the Event

Basketball is currently played between two teams of five—two guards, two forwards, and a center. Substitutions may be made at any break in the action, and substituted players may return any time the clock is stopped.

Games last 40 minutes, played in 20-minute halves. Play begins at the center circle with the referee and one player from each team. The referee tosses the ball, and the two players leap up and attempt to tip it to one of their teammates outside the circle. When the offensive team gains possession of the ball, it has 30 seconds to take a shot. Players move the ball into a position close to the basket by dribbling or passing it to a teammate.

A ball that goes through the basket is called a field goal (or basket) and counts as two points. Players take free throws, awarded after a foul, from behind a line 15 feet (4.57 meters) from the basket. A successful free throw scores one point. Long-range shots into the basket from behind a semicircle 20.5 ft (6.25 m) from the basket count for three points. After a basket, an opposing player throws the ball in from the end line and play resumes.

In the Olympics

Men's basketball has been part of the Olympics since 1936. The first Olympic basketball games were played outdoors, in Berlin, on a clay and sand court. The day of the final match, between the United States and Canada, heavy rain turned the court to mud. The United States beat Canada 19-8, and James Naismith presented gold medals to the winners.

The United States won the first seven Olympic basketball tournaments, from 1936 to 1968. With an amazing 62-game winning streak going into the 1972 games, the Americans lost the title to the team from the Soviet Union. In the final seconds of the game, Doug Collins of the United States sank two free throws to put the United States ahead for the first time, 50-49. The Soviets in-bounded the ball and time ran out. The Americans, thinking they had won, began to celebrate. But then officials decided to reset the clock, giving the

HELP FROM THE DEAD

In 1992, Lithuania, which had recently gained its independence from the Soviet Union, had lacked the money to buy uniforms for the games. The team's star player, Sarunas Marciulionis, convinced the Grateful Dead, the band known for its specially dyed clothing, to donate tie-dyed warm-up suits. The uniforms seemed to have inspired the team, which took home the bronze medal.

Michael Jordan, playing for the Dream Team in 1992, was a lead scorer for what many consider to be the greatest basketball team ever assembled.

Soviets another three seconds to score. The Soviets made the most of their second chance. Ivan Edeshko threw a long pass to Alexander Belov, who pushed past two defenders, caught the ball, and scored to give his team a 51-50 victory. Although the United States filed an official protest, the decision was final.

Ever since losing to the Soviet Union in 1972, the Americans had been waiting for a chance to settle the score. In 1988, the two rivals met in the semifinals. The U.S. team included future NBA stars David Robinson, Mitch Richmond, and Danny Manning. But it was not enough to make the difference. The Soviets, led by their own star players, Arvydas Sabonis and Sarunas Marciulionis, built up a 10-point lead by halftime and coasted to an 82-76 victory. The Soviets went on to beat Yugoslavia and take their second gold medal in basketball.

The greatest basketball star of 1988 games was on neither the Soviet nor the U.S. team. Oscar Schmidt of Brazil set an Olympic record by scoring 55 points in a preliminary-round loss to Spain. He had averaged better than 42 points a game for the entire tournament. By that time, it was apparent to the United States that players in the rest of the world were improving. More than a few times, other countries had assembled teams that could challenge, and even beat, U.S. collegiate players. In 1992, the United States sent its "Dream Team" of NBA players to Barcelona. This was the first year professional players were allowed to play in the Olympics. The Dream Team included Michael Jordan, Larry Bird, and Magic Johnson. Taking the gold seemed like child's play. The team won all of its games by an average of 44 points. The real competition at the 1992 tournament was the battle for second place. The silver medal went to

Croatia, which had on its roster the future NBA players Toni Kukoc, Drazen Petrovic, and Dino Radja.

The U.S. men's team survived a close call before taking the gold at the 2000 games in Sydney, Australia. Lithuania nearly pulled off a gigantic upset, finally falling to the United States 85-83 in the semifinal game. In the final seconds of the game, Lithuania had the ball and a chance to win or tie. An attempt at a three-pointer fell short, however, and the United States went on to defeat France in the final game of the tournament.

Women's basketball made its first appearance at the Olympics in 1976, when the Soviet Union won the women's gold medal. The United States took the silver and Bulgaria earned the bronze. Uljana Semjonova, high scorer for the Soviet women, stood nearly 6 feet 11 inches tall, the tallest female gold medalist ever. She towered over opponents and averaged 19 points and 12 rebounds per game, even though she rarely played more than half of any game. With U.S. women boycotting the 1980 Olympics, Semjonova was again the high scorer, averaging 22 points a game.

The American women's team cruised through the 1984 Olympic tournament, winning all of its games by 28 points or more to carry home the gold. In 1988, the American women defeated Yugoslavia 77-70 for the gold medal. The victorious U.S. team was led by point guard Teresa Edwards and her former University of Georgia teammate Katrina McClain, who led the team in scoring and rebounding.

After winning the gold in 1984 and 1988, anything less than a three-peat in 1992 would have been a surprise. But in the semifinal round, the United States lost to the Unified Team, made up of players from the former Soviet republics. Bitterly disappointed, the Americans went home and assembled a national squad to prepare for the 1996 games. Their hard work and determination paid off in Atlanta, where the U.S. women were never seriously challenged. The team, which featured Lisa Leslie, Katrina McClain, and Teresa Edwards, won every game by at least 12 points.

The U.S. women's team for the 2000 games in Sydney included Lisa Leslie, Sheryl Swoopes, and five-time Olympian Teresa Edwards. The Americans took six out of six games, beating the Australians 76-54 for the gold medal.

RETIRED AT 36

Teresa Edwards, who has won four gold medals, is the most decorated Olympic basketball player ever. She played in several memorable games, particularly one against Cuba in the 1992 games. During that game, Edwards made seven 3-pointers. During the game against Australia in 1996, she made a record 15 assists.

Edwards played 214 basketball games in the red, white, and blue uniform of the USA. As one sportswriter noted, "No one who ever laced on a pair of sneakers has given more for her country."

BOXING

Olympic boxers generally win by outscoring their opponents. Judges award points based on the number of fair, clean punches a fighter lands on his opponent. Boxers are sometimes called pugilists, from the Latin word for "a person who fights with his fists."

Origin of the Sport

Modern boxing began in England in the early 1700s, when James Figg opened a boxing school in London. At the time, the sport was bare-knuckle fighting. Boxers fought without resting until one fighter quit. Jack Broughton published the first boxing rules in 1743, which stated that a fight was over when one man was knocked down and unable to rise within 30 seconds. In the 1800s, John Graham Chambers, a Cambridge University athlete, wrote another set of rules, and Sir John Sholto Douglas, the eighth Marquis of Queensbury, published them. These so-called Queensbury rules required boxers to wear gloves and called for rounds to be three minutes long, with a one-minute rest period between each round. The rules also stated that a man who had been knocked down had ten seconds to get back up on his feet. With only a few changes, the Queensbury rules are still used in professional boxing.

Fast Facts

First Olympic competition

St. Louis, Missouri, USA; 1904

Legendary athletes

Felix Savon, **Cuba**

Teófilo Stevenson, **Cuba**

Criteria for winning

Highest score

Cassius Clay, later known as Muhammad Ali, won the light heavyweight title at the 1960 games in Rome.

Competing in the Event

Olympic bouts last up to four rounds, each lasting two minutes. Olympic boxers compete in 12 weight classes, from light-flyweight (106 pounds/48 kilograms) to super-heavyweight (more than 201 lb/91 kg).

Judges award points after each round. Three clean, fair blows equal one point. A boxer can win a fight in four ways. A knockout (KO) occurs when one fighter is knocked down and is unable to rise within ten seconds. Knockouts are rare in the Olympics. Most fighters win by outscoring their opponents. A technical knockout (TKO) is awarded when a fighter is hurt and unable to continue, such as when he is still standing but appears to be dazed. He has eight seconds to resume fighting. Three 8-counts in a round, or four in a fight, result in a TKO. A boxer may also win by decision. After a fight goes the full four rounds with neither fighter knocked down, the five judges render a decision.

Fouls result in point deductions. Fouls include hitting below the belt, kicking or head butting, using offensive language, and displaying aggressive behavior toward the referee. A boxer may be disqualified after a referee has given him three foul warnings.

In the Olympics

One of the world's oldest sports, boxing was part of the games in ancient Greece. The sport was excluded from the first modern Olympics in 1896, because it was considered dangerous and ungentlemanly. It was included, however, in the 1904 games in St. Louis, Missouri.

Cuba's TEÓFILO STEVENSON became the first boxer to win three Olympic gold medals in the same division. He won the super-heavyweight title in 1972, 1976, and 1980. More than a decade later, Cuban heavyweight Felix Savon matched Stevenson's feat, winning gold medals in 1992, 1996, and 2000.

The United States has won more Olympic boxing medals than any other country—a total of 110. In 1976, the Spinks brothers, Leon and Michael, won two of America's five gold medals. Leon took the light-heavyweight gold and Michael captured the middleweight gold.

SPRINGBOARD TO THE PROS

Boxing is one of the last Olympic sports open only to amateurs. Many of the all-time great American boxers have used the Olympics as a springboard into professional boxing:

Floyd Patterson (1952 middleweight/gold)

Joe Frazier (1964 heavyweight/gold)

George Foreman (1968 heavyweight/gold)

Sugar Ray Leonard (1976 light-welterweight/gold)

Pernell Whitaker (1984 lightweight/gold)

Mark Breland (1984 welterweight/gold)

Virgil Hill (1984 middleweight/silver)

Riddick Bowe (1988 super-heavyweight/silver)

Oscar de la Hoya (1992 lightweight/gold)

CANOEING

The events of the Olympic program for canoe and kayak are classified by the type of boat (Canadian canoe or kayak) and number of paddlers, and also by the type of water paddled (flatwater or whitewater). Canoeists kneel in open boats, which they propel with a single-bladed paddle. Kayakers, on the other hand, sit in closed boats. They use paddles with blades at both ends to propel their craft while controlling a steering rudder with their feet.

Origin of the Sport

Canoes and kayaks have been an important means of travel for thousands of years. The first canoes and kayaks were constructed from available materials. In the Pacific Northwest, for example, where trees were very large and plentiful, Native Americans carved their canoes out of whole tree trunks. These sturdy boats could carry as many as 50 people. In the Arctic, where trees were scarce, the Inuit constructed kayaks by attaching sealskin to a framework of whalebone or driftwood. Today, these crafts are made from light, durable materials, such as aluminum and fiberglass.

John MacGregor, an English lawyer, receives credit for introducing canoeing as recreational sport. In the mid-1800s, he designed a boat based on the Inuit kayak. Between 1845 and 1869, he took the boat, which he called *Rob Roy*, on trips throughout Europe. He wrote a popular series of books about these journeys, and in 1866 he founded the Royal Canoe Club. Two events in 1924—the formation of the Internationella för Kanotidrott (IRK) in Copenhagen and an international regatta in Paris—brought the sport closer to the Olympic Games. The regatta was a great success, and IRK embarked on a campaign to make canoeing an Olympic sport. Nearly 12 years later, the IOC admitted canoeing for the 1936 games in Berlin.

Competing in the Event

Twelve of the 16 Olympic events are flatwater races—straight-ahead sprints on a calm, straight course with marked lanes. The lanes are 9 meters (29.5 feet) wide. Boats must

Fast Facts

First Olympic competition

Berlin, Germany; 1936

Legendary athletes

Gert Fredriksson, **Sweden**

Birgit Schmidt Fischer, **Germany**

Criteria for winning

Fastest time

stay in the their lanes and may not come within 5 m (16.4 ft) of another boat. Each boat is allowed one false start. A second false start results in disqualification.

Because of design restrictions, all the crafts are the same. The speed and endurance of the athletes determine the outcome of the race. Men compete in 500-m and 1,000-m sprints in singles and doubles kayaks, and in singles and doubles canoes. They also compete in a 4-person kayak race of 1,000 m. Women compete in 500-m races in 1-, 2-, and 4-person kayaks.

The whitewater portions of the Olympic events occur on a slalom course constructed to resemble wild river conditions. The course is marked off by a series of gates suspended above the waterway. Whitewater events are similar to the slalom events in Alpine skiing in the Winter Games. The course is about 415 m (454 yards) long and has 20 to 25 gates, of which at least 6 must be negotiated upstream. The last gate is 25 m (27 yds) from the finish line.

Whitewater paddlers need tremendous strength and skill to navigate the course of obstacles and swirling water. Competitors paddle the course one boat at a time, and the fastest time wins. Touching a gate adds 5 seconds to a paddler's time; missing a gate adds 50 seconds. Each competitor runs the course twice, and the better of the two runs counts for scoring purposes.

Whitewater kayakers must have both agility and strength to make it through the challenging obstacle course.

In the Olympics

Canoeing was first included at the 1936 Summer Olympics in Berlin, Germany. The program consisted primarily of long-distance flatwater races. The debut event was a great success, with 19 nations participating. The 27 medals were awarded to 8 countries, most notably Austria, Holland, Germany, Czechoslovakia, Sweden, and Canada. Women first entered the Olympic canoeing competitions in 1948.

Sweden's Gert Fredriksson won the 1,000-m kayak sprint race three consecutive times between 1948 and 1956. Fredriksson's last Olympic competition was in 1960 in Rome, Italy. He finished his Olympic career with a total of six gold medals, one silver medal, and one bronze medal. He returned four years later as coach of the Swedish team, which took home two gold medals.

Slalom racing was included at the 1972 games in Munich, Germany. That year, James McEwan earned the first Olympic whitewater medal for the United States, taking home the bronze medal in the slalom, while the Soviets swept nearly all the flatwater events. New Zealand burst on the scene at the Los Angeles games in 1984 and won four gold medals—three of which went to Ian Ferguson.

That same year, U.S. kayaker Greg Barton won the bronze medal in the 1,000-meter event. Barton, who was born with two club feet that required surgery, came back in 1988 to beat Australian paddler Grant Davies by 0.005 of a second. Barton was the first U.S. kayaker to win Olympic gold.

Perhaps the greatest paddler in Olympic history, man or woman, is Birgit Schmidt Fischer from the former East Germany. During her 20-year Olympic career, from 1980 to 2000, Fischer won more medals than anyone else. Her total of ten includes seven gold and three silver medals. Fischer was only 18 years old when she won the 500-m kayak event and became the youngest athlete ever to win an Olympic canoeing event. Then in 1996, Fischer was a member of the German team that won the kayak fours 500-m, which made her the first woman in any Olympic sport to win gold medals 16 years apart. The amazing Birgit Fischer won two more gold medals in Sydney: two-person kayak and four-person kayak.

CYCLING

Cycling is so commonplace that it tends to be overlooked as a competitive sport. An Olympic event since 1896, cycling is more than just pedaling with lightning speed. It also involves strategy and endurance.

Origin of the Sport

The bicycle was invented in the early 1790s. The earliest model had no pedals and no steering mechanism. In 1816, German baron Karl von Drais constructed a handlebar to aid in steering. In 1839, Kirkpatrick McMillan, a blacksmith from Scotland, built a bicycle with pedals, which led to the chain-and-sprocket drive of today's cycles. The 1880s brought additional technical improvements, such as solid rubber tires and gears.

People began racing bicycles as far back as the 1860s. Racing on open roads attracted crowds of spectators. Gathered on the roadsides, however, these observers could watch only a portion of the race. Race organizers and promoters realized that money could be made if spectators could see the entire race. Soon indoor tracks, called velodromes, were built. Although auto racing replaced bicycles in the United States, cycling continues to be popular in Europe, which is where almost all of the major road races take place.

Competing in the Event

There are two types of bicycle races—road races and track races. Men and women compete separately in road races. Men race about 17 laps around an 8-mile (12.8-kilometer) course for a total distance of some 136 miles (217.6 km). Women race about 10 laps for a distance of some 80 miles (128 km).

Road races begin with a mass start and cyclists spend most of the race riding in a pack. Pack racing facilitates drafting, a strategy in which a cyclist rides directly behind another cyclist. The first rider blocks the wind, enabling the second rider to move more easily and to save energy for a big push later in the race.

Fast Facts

First Olympic competition

Athens, Greece; 1896

Legendary athletes

Jens Fiedler, Germany

Jeanne Longo, France

Erika Salumäe, Soviet Union

Criteria for winning

Fastest time

Time trials are ridden both on roads and on the track. The time trial, known as the race of truth, is the most difficult cycling event. There is little strategy and no teamwork in time trials; competitors just go all out for the entire distance. Riders are not allowed to draft, so their greatest challenge is wind resistance. An aerodynamic position, similar to a skier's tuck, enables the cyclist to cut through the air with as little wind resistance as possible. Men ride four laps of the road course, which is about 32.5 miles (52 km); women ride two laps, or about 16.2 miles (26 km). Cyclists start at one- or two-minute intervals and ride solo over the course. The rider with the fastest time wins.

Track races are held on a velodrome, which is a wooden oval with banked curves, 250 meters around. Track-racing bikes have only one gear and no brakes. There are four different kinds of track races: match sprint, pursuit, points race, and time trial.

In the match sprint, racers compete two at a time for four laps, or 1,000 m. For the first 800 m the cyclists circle the track, carefully maneuvering for position, usually trying to avoid taking the lead so that they can take advantage of drafting. Sometimes two riders will come to an almost complete stop on the track in the hope of forcing the other rider to take the lead. With about 200 m left in the race, they sprint toward the finish line. Only this last stretch of the race

The 3,000-meter individual competition for women was introduced at the 1992 games in Barcelona. American cyclist Rebecca Twigg took home the bronze medal in the event.

is timed. The match sprint is a very tactical race. With no lane markings, riders use the entire width of track, often diving from the top of the embankment to gain momentum.

In individual pursuit races, two cyclists start on opposite sides of the track and literally chase each other around the track. A cyclist wins by catching and passing the other cyclist, or by recording the fastest time. Race strategies vary. Some riders start slowly and hope to catch those who start fast but then tire and slow down. Other riders sprint at the start to break away from the opponent. The team pursuit race is similar to the individual pursuit, except that a four-person team rides around the track in single file as a unit. The winner of the race is determined when the third member of the winning team crosses the finish line.

The points race is an action-packed event that is difficult to follow because the race is essentially 20 races in 1. Cyclists ride 100 laps around the track. Every fifth lap is a sprint lap. Points are awarded to the riders who finish the lap in first, second, third, and fourth places. Double points are awarded on the final lap. The rider with the most points wins.

In the Olympics

The first modern Olympiad featured six cycling events for men. France outpedaled the other nations and won four gold medals. Since that time, France has taken a total of 84 medals, 37 of them gold. Italy, in second place, has won 56 medals, including 33 gold. The United States has won 40 medals, including 11 gold.

The men's road race has given cycling fans many memorable moments. At the 1912 Olympics, the road race was a grueling 320 km (199 miles). The race began at 2:00 A.M., and competitors were sent out on the course at 2-minute intervals over 4 hours. The winner was Rudolph Lewis of South Africa, who posted a time of 10 hours 42 minutes 39 seconds.

In 1920, six railway crossings intersected the course. Timekeepers were stationed at each crossing to keep track of any delays caused by a passing train. The first cyclist to cross the finish line was Henry Kaltenbrun of South Africa, who was greeted with a victory celebration. It was later discovered, however, that Sweden's Harry Stenquist had waited

MOUNTAIN BIKING

Mountain biking began in California in the 1970s and became an Olympic sport for men and women in 1996. Most mountain-bike races—which test bike-handling skills and endurance—are on forest roads, fields, earth, and gravel paths. Many mountain bikers sprint at the start of the race to break away from the pack. They know it will be difficult to pass on the narrow trails ahead. Others start slowly, planning to overtake the fast starters later in the race. Italy's Paola Pezzo won the gold medals for the women's mountain-biking event in both 1996 and 2000. In the men's race, Miguel Martinez of France won the bronze in 1996 and the gold in 2000.

four minutes at a railway crossing. When that delay was subtracted from his time, Stenquist became the clear winner.

Cyclists will do anything for an edge. In 1976, the West German cyclists filled their tires with helium, which is lighter than air. They were not allowed to wear their one-piece silk bodysuits, however, because of the unfair aerodynamic advantage the suits would have given them. Cyclists made a new fashion statement in the early 1980s, when Darth Vader helmets and rubberized skin suits were allowed in competition. Specially designed aerodynamic bicycles debuted at the 1984 games. These sophisticated cycles, made of fiberglass and Kevlar, weigh as little as seven pounds. The use of disc wheels further reduces wind resistance, thus increasing speed.

Germany's Jens Fiedler became the first cyclist to win gold medals in individual events at successive Olympiads when he won the match sprint races in 1992 and 1996. Both times, it took a photo-finish camera to decide the victor. In 1992, Fiedler won the race by about two inches. In 1996, Fiedler won the first race against the USA's Marty Nothstein by even less distance—one centimeter. Nothstein went on to beat Fiedler at the 2000 games in Sydney, Australia. Nothstein's triumph was the first Olympic gold in cycling for the United States since 1984.

Women's cycling became an Olympic event in 1984, when an individual road race was held. That year, the United States captured gold and silver medals as Connie Carpenter-Phinney edged ahead of her teammate Rebecca Twigg at the last second. In 1988, a women's track race was added, and Connie Paraskevin-Young earned the bronze, which was the only cycling medal the United States won in Seoul.

Erika Salumäe of the Soviet Union won the first women's match sprint in 1988. She turned in another gold-medal performance in 1992, this time as a member of the Estonian team.

Many people consider Jeanne Longo of France the greatest women's cyclist ever. By the summer of 1996, she had won ten world championships. An Olympic gold medal still eluded her, however. In 1992, Longo was disappointed with a second-place finish in the road race. Her perseverance paid off with a gold medal in the event in 1996, then a bronze in the individual time trial in 2000.

DIVING

Diving is one of the most graceful sports in the Olympics. Divers perform gravity-defying twists and turns in the air before plunging into a pool with hardly a splash. Divers, like gymnasts, must be strong and flexible. Timing and form are critical.

Origin of the Sport

References to diving appear in ancient literature and art. A wall painting in Naples, dating from the 400s B.C., shows a man diving from a high platform. Diving developed as a sport in the 1600s when German and Swedish gymnasts began to practice their moves at the beach. In the late 1800s, early exhibitions of so-called "fancy diving" from a 10-meter platform led to the formation of the Amateur Diving Association, the world's first official diving organization.

The popularity of diving in the United States owes much to Ernst Bransten and Mike Peppe. Bransten came to the United States from Sweden in the 1920s and introduced Americans to Swedish diving techniques. Peppe coached at Ohio State University in the early 1930s and produced many national college champions.

Diving has been on the Olympic program almost since the start of the modern games. Platform diving appeared for the first time at the 1904 games in St. Louis, and springboard was added at the 1908 games in London. Both events were for men only until 1912, when platform for women was added. Women's springboard came in 1920.

Competing in the Event

Height is one of the main distinctions between platform and springboard diving. The diving platform is a stationary surface about 33 feet (10 meters) above the surface of the pool. Divers reach it by climbing a ladder. The surface of the platform measures about 20 ft (6 m) long and 6.5 ft (2 m) wide. The water below is about 18 ft (5.4 m) deep.

The fulcrum that supports the springboard gives flexibility to the board and a springy lift to the diver. This enables

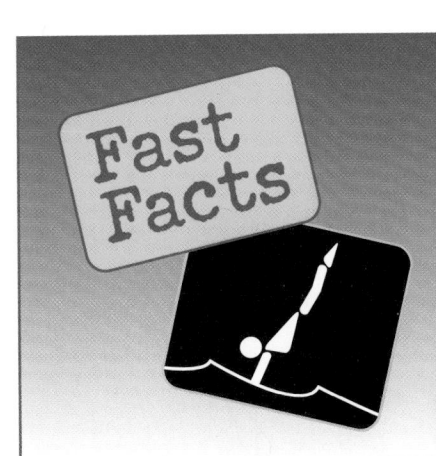

Fast Facts

First Olympic competition

St. Louis, Missouri; 1904

Legendary athletes

Klaus Dibiasi, Italy
Greg Louganis, USA
Patricia McCormick, USA
Fu Mingxia, China

Criteria for winning

Highest score

BREAKING THE RECORD

Inspired by Greg Louganis, a former high school wrestler named Mark Lenzi began diving in 1986. Five years later, Lenzi became the first diver to score more that 100 points on a single dive, beating Louganis's 99-point record. Lenzi was also the first springboard diver to successfully execute a 4.5 somersault in competition.

the diver to jump high off the board and perform complex maneuvers in the air before piercing the water's surface. The springboard is 16 ft (4.8 m) long, 20 inches (50.8 centimeters) wide, and about 9.8 ft (3 m) above the surface of the water. The board extends about 6 ft (1.8 m) out over the water. Springboards, which used to be made of wood, are now made of aluminum. Because aluminum springboards are more flexible, divers have greater lift and, thus, more time to perfect each dive.

Olympic diving competitions consist of preliminary, semifinal, and final rounds. The top divers in each round advance to the next round. In each round, competitors make a number of required dives and optional dives. Divers may select their own program from the 82 springboard and 87 platform dives that the International Diving Federation, the governing body of the sport, recognizes as acceptable.

Dives are rated on their degree of difficulty, which can be from 1.1 to 3.6. The tougher the dive, the more points a diver can score if he or she performs it well. Judges award scores between 0 and 10 points for each dive. In determining their score, judges analyze various elements, such as approach, takeoff, elevation, execution, and entry. The best and worst scores are tossed out, and the remaining are added together. That figure is then multiplied by the degree of difficulty, and the new total is multiplied by 0.6 to produce the diver's final score.

There are six basic dives: forward, back, reverse, inward, twisting, and arm stand (platform only). Competitors execute these dives from four positions: tuck, pike, straight, and free (diver's choice). In the tuck position, the diver's body is bent at the waist and knees, with the legs pulled tight to the chest. Legs are straight in the pike position and the body is bent at the waist. With more than 85 basic dives and 4 positions, the diver can choose from more than 330 variations.

In the Olympics

Divers from Germany and Sweden dominated the early Olympic aquatic events. Since the mid-1980s, however, China has become an international diving powerhouse. In recent Olympiads, Chinese divers won 22 of 48 medals, including five gold and five silver medals at the Sydney games in 2000.

Despite the strong competition, U.S. athletes have been the most consistent diving performers. In platform, U.S. divers have taken 12 of 23 gold medals in the men's competition and 9 of 20 in the women's event. In springboard, the American team has won 16 of 21 gold medals in men's and 11 of 19 in women's competition. Between 1920 and 2000, American men won the gold medal in the springboard event in all but three Olympiads. American men also captured the springboard silver medal in every Olympiad from 1920 to 1964. During that time, the Americans swept the springboard event, giving up only three bronze medals. Vladimir Vasin of the former Soviet Union broke the Americans' winning streak by taking the springboard gold in 1972, which was the first diving medal for his country.

Italy's Klaus Dibiasi is believed to be Europe's most successful diver ever. He won the men's platform gold medal in three straight Olympiads—1968, 1972, and 1976. He also won two Olympic silver medals—platform in 1964 and springboard in 1968.

After winning the gold in platform in 1948 and 1952, American diver Sammy Lee continued his diving career as a coach. His student GREG LOUGANIS is considered by many to be the best diver in history. Louganis won four gold medals and one silver medal in Olympic competition. He was also the first male diver to win both the springboard and the platform events in two consecutive Olympics (1984 and 1988).

Women's platform diving first appeared on the Olympic program in 1912 at the Stockholm games. Women's springboard was added in 1920. American Aileen Riggin (then 14 years old) won a gold medal in 1920 and a silver medal in 1924, both for springboard. She also captured a bronze

Performing in pairs, synchronized divers must be perfectly timed in height and distance from the platform, speed of rotation, and angle of entry into the water.

LESS IS MORE

Some Chinese divers who are recruited have never even seen a swimming pool. Chinese coaches look for athletes who are short and compact, and who may have hyperextended elbows (elbows that touch when the person's arms are raised above the head). With hyperextended elbows, a diver can enter the water with less of a splash, thus gaining a higher score.

swimming medal in backstroke at the 1924 games. Elizabeth Becker of the United States was the first woman to win two diving titles—the springboard gold in 1924 and the platform gold in 1928. Another American diver, Victoria Draves, swept the gold in the springboard and platform events in 1948 and became the first woman to accomplish that feat. Patricia McCormick of the United States was the first diver to win springboard and platform gold medals at two different Olympiads. She won her medals in 1952 and 1956. Carrying on the family tradition, Pat's daughter Kelly won the silver medal in the springboard competition in 1984 and a bronze medal in springboard at the 1988 games.

Until 1980, the only non-American to win the women's springboard event was East German diver Ingrid Kramer, who triumphed in springboard and platform in 1960 and repeated for the springboard gold in 1964. Then the springboard title came back to the United States with victories by Sue Gossick (1968), Micki King (1972), and Jennifer Chandler (1976).

An American woman won the platform gold medals from 1924 to 1956. In 1952 and 1956, the U.S. women made a clean sweep of all six Olympic platform medals. Leslie Bush, a 17-year-old from New Jersey, regained the title for the American team in 1964, but then Olympic gold eluded the U.S. women until Laura Wilkinson won the platform title in 2000. Wilkinson, who was in fifth place, 60 points behind, nailed her last three dives to overtake silver medalist Li Na of China.

When Fu Mingxia of China was only 14 years old, she turned in a stunning performance that won the platform gold medal at the 1992 Summer Olympics in Barcelona, Spain. She repeated her success in 1996 in Atlanta and then retired from diving to enter college in Beijing. Four years later, Fu Mingxia returned to the Olympics. She won the springboard title and became the first female diver to win five career medals.

The IOC added synchronized diving to the roster of events for the 2000 games in Sydney. Pairs of divers, chosen from among those who qualified as individuals for their country's team, performed in unison from both springboard and platform.

EQUESTRIAN

Equestrian competition tests the level of control and communication between a rider and a horse. Equestrian consists of dressage (in which the horse performs a series of prescribed movements) and jumping (in which the horse and rider jump a series of obstacles in the shortest possible time). It is the only Olympic sport in which men and women compete against each other on an equal basis.

Origin of the Sport

Ancient peoples domesticated horses before the early Olympic Games. At first, people used horses to carry heavy loads. Eventually, the Scythians (nomads from present-day Russia, Ukraine, and Kazakhstan) developed the equestrian arts and some types of equipment that are still used today. As riding academies opened in Italy, France, and Austria in the 1500s, modern equestrian competition developed. Horses were trained to perform various movements and jumps that were important to cavalry soldiers who rode horses in battle.

The earliest equestrian competitions took place in Europe, Great Britain, Russia, and the United States. At first, only cavalry officers competed. Since the 1950s, however, the sport has been open to everyone.

Competing in the Events

Olympic equestrian athletes compete in three events: dressage, show jumping, and three-day eventing. Each event has both individual and team competitions. In team events, four horses and four riders from each country compete. Participants must be at least 18 years old for the three-day and jumping events, and 16 years old for dressage. Age requirements also exist for the horses, which must be at least 7 years old. Riders use the standard English saddle and wear formal riding jackets, or uniforms if they are in the military. For the jumping events, riders wear helmets; for dressage, they wear top hats.

In the dressage competition, the horse and rider perform a series of 36 different movements, such as walk, trot, change

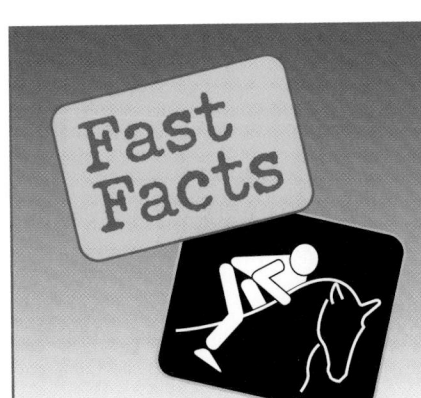

Fast Facts

First Olympic competition

Paris, France; 1900

Legendary athletes

Reiner Klimke, **Germany**

John Michael Plumb, **USA**

Nicole Uphoff, **Germany**

Hans-Gunter Winkler, **Germany**

Criteria for winning

Highest score

SECOND CAREER

Several gold medalists have used their Olympic success as a spring-board to a career in the movies. One Olympian to do so was Cornishman V, the horse that helped two different riders win medals in 1968 and 1972. Cornishman V appeared in two movies—*Dead Cert* (1974) and *International Velvet* (1978).

of pace and direction, and stop. The prescribed moves are executed in silence. Casual viewers may feel that dressage lacks the excitement of other equestrian events, but the beauty and perfection of the event are helping the sport gain popularity. For each movement, judges award points ranging from 0 to 10. The judges look for the versatility, obedience, flexibility, rhythm, and training of the horse. Scores are also based on the rider's form and control, and how eagerly the horse performs. Riders and horses receive penalty points for errors.

Show jumping is thrilling to watch. Riders guide their mounts through 12 to 20 obstacles that the horse must jump. The obstacles include walls, poles, gates, and water. Speed is important, but horse and rider are penalized for each obstacle the horse touches or knocks down. The rider with the fastest time (and usually the fewest penalty points) wins.

Three-day eventing consists of dressage, show jumping, and endurance. The endurance phase is a cross-country race over a 17- to 20-mile (27 to 32 kilometers) course. The course has four sections, which can include roads, tracks, fields, and obstacles.

In the Olympics

Historic evidence suggests that equestrian events were included in the ancient Olympic Games of 648 B.C. In modern times, equestrian competitions have been part of the games since 1900. During most of this time, Germany has dominated the event, capturing a record 72 medals. The dressage event, in which only commissioned officers competed from 1912 to 1952, was almost won by Sweden in 1948. One member of the team was disqualified because of his lack of rank, however, and the team lost its medal.

Women and civilians entered the equestrian competitions in 1952. That year Lis Hartel of Denmark won the silver medal even though her legs were paralyzed from polio. She had to be helped on and off her horse. Four years later, Hartel competed again and took the silver in dressage.

As Swedish athletes were winning gold medals, German riders were beginning to emerge as an equestrian power to be reckoned with. Reiner Klimke of West Germany began a series of amazing victories that included team golds in 1964,

1968, 1976, 1984, and 1988; the individual bronze in 1968 and 1976; and the individual gold in 1984.

For the first time ever, women captured all three dressage medals at the 1988 games in Seoul—Nicole Uphoff (Germany, gold); Margit Otto-Crépin (France, silver); and Christine Stückelberger (Switzerland, bronze). Uphoff won again in 1992 and became the only woman ever to win two individual Olympic gold medals in dressage. Her teammates won the silver and bronze. Not since 1912, when the Swedes outclassed their rivals, had any nation swept the individual dressage medals.

Show jumping in the Olympics began in 1912, when the gold medal went to French military officer Jean Cariou. For the next 40 years, military men dominated the Olympic medals. The first civilian to capture a medal was Pierre Jonqueres d'Oriola of France, who took the individual gold in 1952.

Demonstrating its skill in show jumping, Germany took four gold medals from 1956 to 1972. The most notable member of the team during that period was Hans-Gunter Winkler, who won a record seven Olympic medals, including one individual gold (1956) and four team golds (1956, 1960, 1964, and 1972), a team silver (1976), and a team bronze (1968).

Sweden and the Netherlands dominated the three-day events until the 1940s. The U.S. equestrian team has also enjoyed a measure of success in the three-day event. Americans have earned a total of four silver and two bronze individual medals. In the team competition, the United States has won three golds, four silvers, and a bronze. John Michael Plumb won six Olympic medals, including an individual silver, in the three-day event, which is a record for an American rider in that competition.

The spectacular sight of horses leaping through the air makes show jumping the most exciting event of the equestrian competition.

FENCING

Fencing is a sport of attack and defense using swords. It is a series of strategic moves and counter-moves. Fencing is the only combative sport in the Olympics that has neither height restrictions nor weight classifications.

Origin of the Sport

Like archery and javelin, fencing has its roots in early armed combat. People have been using swords for defense for thousands of years. The first evidence of a fencing match is an Egyptian carving from around 1100 B.C. that shows two men fighting with swords. They are wearing masks similar to those used today and are being observed by a panel of judges.

Swordsmanship developed in Europe in the 1300s. Until that time warriors wielded swords of increasing weight to penetrate the heavy armor worn by their opponents. With the invention of firearms, armor became obsolete. This led to the development of lighter swords, faster and more intricate handwork, and the art of fencing.

Competing in the Event

The modern fencer uses one of three swords: foil, épée, and sabre. Until 1996, women competed only in foil. The dueling surface, which is called a piste, is 2 meters (6 feet, 7 inches) wide. It is 14 m (46 ft) long for foil and 18 m (59 ft) long for épée and sabre.

To protect themselves from injuries, fencers wear wire-mesh masks, thick canvas or nylon jackets and knickers, and a padded glove on the hand that holds the sword. Since the introduction of electronic scoring in the 1930s, fencers also wear a wire linking the weapon to the scoring machine.

Weighing less than a pound, the foil is the lightest of the three swords. Its blade, which measures about 35 inches (89 centimeters) long, is rectangular and flexible. A small, bowl-shaped guard protects the fencer's hand. Foil fencers score by hitting their opponent's torso with the sword tip. Hits to the head, arms, or legs do not count. The fencer who attacks first may score. A defensive block against an attack is called a parry.

Fast Facts

First Olympic competition

Athens, Greece; 1896

Legendary athletes

Aladar Gerevich, **Hungary**

Yelena Novikova,
  Soviet Union

Criteria for winning

First to score five hits

The épée is heavier than the foil and has a stiffer blade. A bell-shaped guard protects the hand. Touches anywhere on the opponent's body count as a point. If both fencers touch each other at the same time, both score a point.

Similar in length, weight, and flexibility to the foil, the sabre has a handguard that curves around to protect the back of the hand. Sabre fencers score points by touching their opponent's torso with either the sword point or one of the two cutting edges.

Fencing matches, called bouts, are six minutes long. The first fencer to score five touches, or hits, wins. If neither fencer reaches that number after six minutes, the competitor with the most hits wins.

In the Olympics

Baron de Coubertin, who is credited with reviving the ancient Olympic Games, was himself a championship fencer. This may be why fencing is one of only six sports that have been in the modern games since 1896.

Hungarians dominated Olympic fencing for 60 years— from 1908 to 1968. Aladar Gerevich was perhaps the greatest fencer in this amazing dynasty. He is the only athlete to win medals in six different Olympiads. Yelena Novikova of the former Soviet Union holds the women's record for gold medals. From 1968 to 1976, she won four gold medals in foil.

French fencer Laura Flessel (left) wins the gold in the women's individual épée competition with this final strike on Valerie Barlois, also of France.

FIELD HOCKEY

Field hockey is a team sport involving speed, power, and agility. Two teams use special sticks to hit a ball into their opponent's goal. In the United States, field hockey is played mostly by girls and women in high schools and colleges. In much of the rest of the world, field hockey is played mostly by men and is as popular as baseball is in the United States.

Origin of the Sport

A drawing in an ancient Egyptian tomb shows a ball-and-stick game similar to field hockey being played more than 4,000 years ago. Historians believe that the ancient Greeks and Romans also played field hockey and that some form of it was played during the Middle Ages. Modern field hockey developed in Great Britain and was first introduced to the Olympics at the 1908 games in London.

Field hockey was introduced in the United States in 1921 by Constance M. K. Applebee, a British teacher who taught the game to women at colleges in the northeast and the mid-Atlantic states. Growing interest in the sport among women led to the formation of the United States Field Hockey Association (USFHA) in 1922. Then, in 1928, the Field Hockey Association of America (FHAA) was founded to govern men's field hockey in the United States. In 1993, the FHAA and the USFHA joined to form a single governing body for the sport.

Competing in the Event

Field hockey is played on a rectangular field, or pitch, measuring 100 yards by 60 yards (91.44 meters by 54.86 meters). Each team consists of five forwards, three halfbacks, two fullbacks, and a goalie who protects a net about the same size as that of a soccer goal. All players wear shin guards; goalies also wear masks and protective padding.

The object of the game is to score more goals than the other team. A player dribbles, passes, and shoots a white, hard, plastic ball with a wooden stick that is curved at the striking end. To score, an offensive player must hit the ball from inside the striking circle—a semicircle 16 yds (14.6 m) in front of the net. A player may also score on a penalty shot, which gives him or her a clear shot at the net, with the goalkeeper as the sole opponent.

Field hockey is played in two 35-minute halves. A time-out is called only when a player has been injured. Play begins at midfield with a pass-back, in which a player from one team hits the ball back to a teammate waiting behind. Play continues as one team passes the ball toward the op-posing goal while the other team tries to defend its goal and to gain control of the ball. All players have an equal opportunity to gain control of the ball as it is dribbled and passed downfield. Obstruction of the ball's movement or shielding the ball from other play-ers with any part of the body is pro-hibited. Only the goalie is allowed to touch or stop the motion of the ball with his or her hands, feet, or body.

Field hockey players dribble, pass, and shoot a ball with the flat side of the curved end of the hockey stick.

In the Olympics

No country has dominated field hockey the way India has. The Indian men's team won six straight Olympic gold medals between 1928 and 1956. A loss to Pakistan in the finals of the 1960 games in Rome, Italy, broke India's 30-game winning streak, which is an Olympic record. India's Dhyan Chand dominated the game from 1928 to 1936. In the 12 Olympic matches in which he played, Chand scored 38 goals. He later became coach of India's national team. During that time In-dia outscored its opposition 197 goals to 8. In 19 Olympiads, the Indian men's team won eight gold medals, one silver, and two bronze. Its gold medals in field hockey are the only gold medals India has won in the Olympic Games.

Women have been playing Olympic field hockey only since 1980, when Zimbabwe unexpectedly won the gold, Czechoslovakia took the silver, and the Soviet Union won the bronze medal.

GYMNASTICS

Gymnastics combines the excitement of acrobatics—vaulting, tumbling, jumping, and twisting—with the grace and precision of dance movements. Judges look for form, balance, and artistic expression in gymnastic performances.

Origin of the Sport

Gymnastics has existed in one form or another since the earliest known sports activities. Evidence suggests that Chinese and Egyptian acrobats performed tumbling and balancing activities before 2000 B.C. Minoan athletes, on the island of Crete off the coast of present-day Greece, performed a spectacular stunt. They grasped the horns of a charging bull and with a front handspring flipped over the animal's head to land on its back. As part of their training, ancient Roman soldiers used wooden horses—forerunners of the pommel horse—to practice mounting and dismounting. During the Middle Ages, acrobats traveled the countryside and made their living as court entertainers.

Modern gymnastics began to develop in the late 1700s and early 1800s. Friedrich Muths and Friedrich Jahn invented some of the gymnastics apparatus that is used today. European immigrants who came to the United States in the 1800s brought the sport with them. Gymnastics clubs and the YMCA promoted the sport, which soon became part of the early physical education programs in American schools. Around 1900, gymnastics declined in popularity as team sports were being emphasized. Then in the 1970s, gymnastics in the United States received a boost, due in large part to the televised Olympic performances of Olga Korbut (Soviet Union, 1972) and NADIA COMANECI (Romania, 1976).

Competing in the Event

Competitive gymnastics consists of two different sports—artistic events for both men and women, and rhythmic gymnastics for women only. Olympic gymnasts compete in three different categories. They are team competition, individual all-around finals, and individual event finals.

Fast Facts

First Olympic competition

Athens, Greece; 1896

Legendary athletes

Nadia Comaneci, Romania

Larysa Latynina, Soviet Union

Mary Lou Retton, USA

Vitaly Scherbo, Belarus

Criteria for winning

Highest score

In the team competition, five athletes perform on each apparatus. In the past, compulsory and optional routines were required of all competitors at a particular level. The compulsory exercises were eliminated after the 1996 games in Atlanta, Georgia. For the optional routines, each athlete composes his or her program individually. Judges look for the degree of difficulty of the moves, as well as their execution. The 36 best athletes from the team competition compete in the individual all-around finals. In the individual event finals, the six best gymnasts on each apparatus compete in team competition optionals.

The men's competition consists of six events: horizontal bar, parallel bars, pommel horse, vault, rings, and floor exercise. The horizontal, or high, bar is a flexible steel bar mounted 7 feet 10 inches (2.4 meters) above the floor. It is used for swinging and vaulting movements. The parallel bars are two flexible wooden rails set about 5 ft 8 inches (1.7 m) above the floor. Athletes perform swings, vaults, balance positions, and presses to handstands on the parallel bars.

The pommel horse is a padded cylinder with two pommels, or handles. Only the athlete's hands can touch the horse, and his movements are swinging and continuous (no

Routines on the balance beam last only 70 to 90 seconds, but they must be performed perfectly or points are lost.

stops are permitted). The vault, or long horse, uses the same apparatus as the pommel horse event, but with the pommels removed. For the competition, the gymnast takes an approach run of about 27 yards (25 m) and vaults the horse lengthwise.

The rings, which are wooden, are spaced 20 inches (50 centimeters) apart. Ring activities include swinging, held positions, and slow movements that emphasize the athlete's strength. The rings must be still throughout the entire performance. Any movement of the rings is penalized. The dismount involves a somersault, with or without a twist. Finally, the floor exercises are performed on a mat and include tumbling, balance, and movements that demonstrate flexibility and strength.

The women's events consist of uneven bars, balance beam, floor exercise, and vault. The uneven parallel bars are similar to the men's parallel bars except that they are set at different heights. Working perpendicular to the bars, gymnasts perform continuous large swinging and vaulting moves. Athletes perform tumbling, balance, and other gymnastic moves on the balance beam. The routine, which lasts more than a minute, must contain at least two flight elements, a 360-degree turn on one foot, and a high leap or jump.

Women use the same mat and area as the men for the floor exercises, but the women perform their routines to music. Continuous movements in the floor routine include tumbling, dance movements, balance positions, and several somersaults. The vaulting horse for women is the one that the men use, except that the vaults are performed across the short dimension of the apparatus. Gymnasts take off from a run and jump off a springboard. Judges look at flight, form, and landing.

In the Olympics

Gymnastics has been an Olympic event for men since the modern Olympic Games began in 1896. Early men's events included rope climbing and club swinging, which were discontinued after the 1932 games. Before World War II, Europeans dominated the competition. Finland, Switzerland, and Italy each won team medals four times.

The former Soviet Union entered Olympic competition in 1952. That, and the rise of Japan as a gymnastics powerhouse, dramatically changed gymnastics competitions. In the dozen or so Olympiads since then, Japan and the former Soviet-bloc countries have dominated men's Olympic gymnastics. Japan won five straight team gold medals from 1960 to 1976. The Soviet Union (and later the Unified Team) won team gold medals in 1952, 1956, 1980, 1988, 1992, and 1996. The United States won the team gold in 1904 and 1984 (the year the Soviet Union boycotted the games).

The men's individual all-around competition has been part of every Olympiad since 1900. Italy's Alberto Braglia was the first all-around champion to win at back-to-back Olympics, in 1908 and 1912. Soviet gymnasts swept the medals in the all-around competition at the 1988 Olympics in Seoul, South Korea. In 1992, VITALY SCHERBO of Belarus became the all-around champion and, two days later, won four straight apparatus finals in addition to the team title to become the first gymnast in history to earn six gold medals at a single Olympiad. Scherbo added four bronze medals in 1996.

American gymnasts swept the medals in the parallel bars event in 1904. The gold medalist, George Eyser, who had a wooden left leg, also won a gold in the vault and the parallel bars, silver medals in the pommel horse and the combined competition, and a bronze in the horizontal bar. It took 80 years for the next American to capture the gold medal in the parallel bars. Bart Conner won the event in 1984. At the 1996 games in Atlanta, Jair Lynch took the silver medal and became the first African-American to win a gymnastics medal.

The pommel horse event was suspended from 1908 to 1920. Heikki Savolainen of Finland captured the bronze medal in 1928, and again 20 years later, in 1948. Savolainen, who set a record by competing in five Olympiads, won two gold, one silver, and six bronze medals during his career. He was 44 years old when he received his last medal as a member of the third-place Finnish team at the Helsinki Olympics.

American gymnast Dallas Bixler won the gold for the horizontal bar event at the 1932 Olympics in Los Angeles. Finnish teammates Heikki Savolainen and Einari Terasvirta tied for second. While the judges discussed a method for

A PERFECT 10

At the Moscow Games in 1980, Aleksandr Dityatin executed a perfect vault and became the first male gymnast to receive a perfect score of 10 from Olympic judges. Dityatin was also the first male gymnast to win medals in eight different events: Gold—Individual Combined, Team, Rings; Silver—Parallel Bars, Horse Vault, Horizontal Bar, Pommel Horse; Bronze—Floor Exercise.

deciding which athlete should receive the silver medal, the two Finns talked it over and agreed that Savolainen should have the silver and Terasvirta the bronze. The judges accepted their decision.

In 1964, Haruhiro Yamashita of Japan won the gold medal for vault with a handspring in a pike position. The new maneuver became known as the Yamashita. In 1972, East Germany's Klaus Koste won the title with a Yamashita and a forward somersault, claiming the first gold for his country in men's gymnastics.

The first Olympic competition for women's gymnastics occurred at the 1928 games in Amsterdam, Holland. The only event was the team competition, which was won by the Netherlands. In 1952, individual events for women on each apparatus were added. The Soviet Union dominated the sport for many years, earning ten team gold medals, including eight consecutive team titles between 1952 and 1980. The United States has won four Olympic team medals—gold in 1996, silver in 1984, and bronze medals in 1948 and 1992. In 1996, American gymnast Kerri Strug supplied the most dramatic moment of the competition when she delivered an amazing performance on a badly sprained ankle. Strug, less than 5 feet tall and weighing just 87 pounds, felt a terrible

Yeng Wei of China, competing on the pommel horse, helped his team win the gold in the men's team finals at the 2000 games in Sydney.

pain shoot up her left ankle after landing short on her first vault. She was about to pass on her second vault, telling her coach Bela Karolyi, "I can't do it. I can't feel my leg." Her teammates, unaware of the severity of her pain, urged Strug to shake it off and to attempt a second vault. Despite the pain, Strug sprinted down the runway, performed the vault and the landing, and then fell to the mat in tears. Her heroic vault earned 9.712 points to clinch the team gold medal for the United States. Minutes later, with her leg in a cast, Strug was carried to the victory podium by her coach.

In 1956, Agnes Keleti (Hungary) and Larysa Latynina (Soviet Union) dominated the individual all-around competition. Keleti had captured gold medals in three of the four apparatus events, but a poor showing on the vault cost her the all-around title. Latynina, who won the competition that year, repeated her triumph in 1960 and took the silver in 1964. During her career as an Olympic athlete, Latynina earned a record-setting 18 medals between 1956 and 1964, including nine gold (a women's Olympic record), five silver, and four bronze medals. Latynina became coach of the Soviet women's team in 1967.

Czechoslovakia's Vera Cáslavská dominated the women's all-around competition in 1964 and again in 1968. In 1968, she won gold medals in the vault, uneven bars, and floor exercise. All together, Cáslavská won seven individual gold medals and four silver medals in Olympic competition. Soviet gymnast Lyudmilla Turischeva won the 1972 all-around championship, but she was overshadowed by her spunky teammate Olga Korbut, who earned three gold medals and a silver medal. Korbut became the first person to perform a back flip on the balance beam, beginning a trend toward more athletic and acrobatic routines for female gymnasts.

The already popular sport received an additional boost at the 1976 games in Montreal, Canada. Fourteen-year-old Nadia Comaneci of Romania became the youngest Olympic all-around champion. (Today, gymnasts must be at least 16 years old to compete in the Olympics.) Comaneci also became the first gymnast to score a perfect ten at the Olympic Games. She earned her first perfect scores on the uneven bars and the balance beam in the team events. By the end of the games, she had earned seven perfect scores and had

HOW IT'S SCORED

The perfect score for any gymnastics event is 10.00, but competitors begin their routines with less than that. Women start with 9.4, and men begin with 9.0. Judges then add bonus points when a gymnast performs especially difficult elements. Each movement is classified according to its degree of difficulty. Judges also subtract points for any errors in the routine or for missing required moves. The highest and lowest scores are dropped, and the final tally is the average of the remaining scores. A gymnast's all-around score is compiled by adding together his or her scores in each event.

RHYTHMIC GYMNASTICS

Rhythmic gymnastics has been an Olympic sport since 1984. Women compete in two events—individual all-around and team combined. Music accompanies the routine, which lasts 75 to 90 seconds.

In the individual events, competitors perform dance steps while manipulating and controlling a ball, hoop, ribbon, rope, or clubs. They roll on the mat, throw the objects into the air, and perform simple acrobatic moves. Gymnasts may not perform flips, cartwheels, or other acrobatic stunts. Judges rate gymnasts on their grace, balance, and flexibility.

walked off with three gold medals, a silver, and a bronze. At the 1980 games in Moscow, Comaneci missed first place by only 0.075 point. That same year, she took the gold in the balance beam and the floor exercise events, as well as the silver in the team competition, giving her an Olympic total of five gold medals, three silver, and one bronze.

At the 1984 games in Los Angeles, 16-year-old MARY LOU RETTON became the first American gymnast to win a gold medal in the all-around competition. With two events remaining, Retton trailed Ecaterina Szabo of Romania by just 0.15 point. Retton earned a perfect ten on the floor exercise, thanks in part to a particularly difficult double back somersault that impressed the judges. To win the gold medal, she then needed a perfect ten in the vault, which she did with style and grace. Her full-twisting layout double Tsukahara—a maneuver that only a few men in the world could manage at the time—was perfect! She had beaten her Romanian rival by only 0.05 point.

At the 1988 Olympics in Seoul, Korea, the all-around championship again came down to the final vault. Russia's Elena Shoushounova scored a perfect ten on her trademark, but risky, full-twisting vault to win the championship over Romanian Daniela Silivas by 0.025 point, the closest-ever women's margin of victory.

Shannon Miller won more medals—five—at the Barcelona games in 1992 than any other American athlete. She won silver medals in the all-around competition and on the balance beam, as well as bronze medals in the uneven bars and floor exercise. Her fifth medal was a bronze medal for the team competition. Miller then added two gold medals in 1996 to become the most decorated American gymnast ever.

The all-around competition swirled with controversy at the 2000 games in Sydney, Australia. Officials had mistakenly set the vault 5 centimeters too low at the start of that event. Because of this error, the favorite in the all-around competition, the former world champion from Russia, Svetlana Khorkina, took a bad tumble on the vault, which cost her the chance of winning the all-around medal. After winning a gold medal in the uneven parallel bars apparatus final three days later, she said, "It will help me to forget that day."

JUDO

Created in Japan in the late 1800s, judo is a martial art that contains elements of the fighting skills of the samurai warriors of the Middle Ages. Translated as "gentle way," judo is based on yielding to an opponent rather than matching strength against strength. An athlete uses the opponent's own moves to pull him or her off balance and into a throw.

Origin of the Sport

Judo is a sporting variation of jujitsu, the hand-to-hand combat favored by medieval samurai warriors, and is used for self-defense. Developed by Dr. Jigoro Kano while he was a student at Tokyo University, judo aims to produce a mental and physical state of harmony and balance through training.

Kano opened his first judo school in 1882 to teach three basic techniques: throwing, groundwork (including pinning holds and strangleholds), and joint locks. Beginning in 1889, Kano traveled abroad to promote judo.

Japan held an All-Japan Championship in 1930, but it was not until the end of World War II that the sport gained an international following. In 1948, the European Judo Union was formed in London, and the first European championships were held three years later. The International Judo Federation, established in 1951, organized the first world championships in Tokyo in 1956.

Early proponents of the sport maintained that it was possible for a smaller athlete to throw a larger one. For this reason, a single competition was open to all male athletes. The success of one 6-foot 6-inch Dutchman against smaller, highly skilled Japanese contestants led to the addition of weight classes in the early 1960s. Today, men and women compete separately in seven weight classes: from extra-light to heavyweight.

Competing in the Event

Judo athletes, called *judoka,* try to throw their opponents, pin them to the mat, or keep them under control by using a hold or lock maneuver. Hitting and kicking are not allowed.

Fast Facts

First Olympic competition

Tokyo, Japan; 1964

Legendary athletes

Anton Geesink, **Holland**
Ryoko Tamura, **Japan**

Criteria for winning

Highest score

A men's match lasts 5 minutes; women's matches are 4 minutes long. Competitors wear baggy pants and a jacket fastened by a colored belt indicating the athlete's rank (white belt is the lowest rank; black belt is the highest). They compete on a square mat measuring 8 to 10 meters (26 to 33 feet) on each side.

After a ceremonial bow between competitors, the referee gives the signal to begin. Contestants step forward and begin to "wrestle" from a standing position, each trying to throw the other and to win a point (called an *ippon*), thus ending the match. An *ippon* can be scored in several ways: by throwing an opponent to the mat, by securing a hold from which an opponent cannot break free for 30 seconds, or by creating a stranglehold or arm lock that forces an opponent to give up. If a match goes full term without an *ippon,* a referee and two judges determine which player's throws and holds were better.

In the Olympics

The host country of the Olympics is generally allowed to include one sport of its own choosing. At the 1964 Olympiad in Tokyo, Japan elected to include judo, although only for men. Japan won three gold medals that year, but Anton Geesink, a 6-foot, 6-inch, 253-pound Dutchman, won the open class (now discontinued) by twice defeating the three-time Japanese champion, Akio Kaminaga (weighing in at 220 lb and standing about 8 inches shorter than Geesink).

Women's judo, introduced as a demonstration sport at the 1988 games in Seoul, Korea, became an official Olympic sport in 1992 at the Barcelona games. Spain captured the gold medals—Miriam Blasco (lightweight) and Almudena Munoz (half-lightweight). That year, Israel's Yael Arad won a silver medal, which was the first Olympic medal in her nation's history, and the French women's team won two gold medals. Japan's Ryoko Tamura won silver medals in 1992 and 1996 and a gold medal in 2000 in the women's extra-lightweight division.

One way to win a point in judo, and end the match, is to throw one's opponent to the mat.

MODERN PENTATHLON

The modern pentathlon is a test of five skills that were required of soldiers—horseback riding, shooting, fencing, swimming, and running. The particular combination of events was based on the assumption that a soldier delivering a message behind enemy lines might have to do these things. He might ride an unfamiliar horse, shoot his way out of a difficult situation, engage in a duel, swim across a raging river, and run through the woods to complete his mission.

Origin of the Sport

Some form of the pentathlon has existed since as far back as 600 B.C. A featured event at the ancient Greek games, it consisted of a sprint, broad jump, javelin throw, discus throw, and wrestling match. Baron Pierre de Coubertin, founder of the modern Olympic Games, created the modern pentathlon and introduced the sport for men at the 1912 Summer Olympics in Stockholm, Sweden. At first, most of the competitors were soldiers and officers. U.S. Army lieutenant George Patton Jr., who became a famous general in World War II, competed in the first Olympic modern pentathlon. He failed to win a medal because, surprisingly, he was a terrible shot with a pistol.

Competing in the Event

Athletes compete in the events in the following order—shooting, fencing, swimming, horseback riding, and running. All five events are held on the same day. Competitors earn points for how well they perform in each event, and the pentathlete with the most points at the end of the competition wins.

Athletes use air pistols to fire pellets at a target 10 meters (32.8 feet) away. The target is 6 inches (15.2 centimeters) in diameter. They take 20 shots at targets that turn to face the shooter at regular intervals. For each shot, a competitor has three seconds to raise, aim, and fire the pistol.

Following the shooting phase, each athlete faces every other competitor in a fencing match using the épée, or

Fast Facts

First Olympic competition	
Stockholm, Sweden; 1912	
Legendary athlete	
Lars Hall, **Sweden**	
Criteria for winning	
Highest score	

Stephanie Cook of Great Britain cheers as she crosses the finish line in the running portion of the modern pentathlon competition at the 2000 games in Sydney.

dueling sword. A competitor must score a touch, or hit, on his opponent within one minute to win the match. If neither fencer scores a touch, both earn a loss.

For the third phase, athletes complete a 200-m (218.8-yard) freestyle swim in a pool. A time of 2 minutes 40 seconds earns 1,000 pentathlon points. For faster times, points are added; for slower times, points are deducted. The swim is followed by an equestrian phase in which competitors ride a horse over a 350- to 450-m (383- to 492-yd) course with 12 jumps. Because the horses are picked at random, this event is one of the toughest. Athletes have only 20 minutes to warm up with their horse.

The pentathlon concludes with a 3-kilometer (1.86-mile) cross-country run. A handicapped start system is used for this final event. This means that the athlete with the most points starts first. Other runners follow at 30-second intervals determined by their ranking in the previous events.

In the Olympics

Swedish athletes have always excelled at the modern pentathlon. From the 1912 Olympics, when the sport was added to the games, to the 1956 games, Swedish athletes took home eight gold, five silver, and four bronze medals. During that time, Lars Hall became the only repeat winner of the event—in 1952 and again in 1956. From 1960 to 2000, Hungarian athletes replaced the Swedes in the top spot by winning the gold in 1960, 1964, 1972, and 1988.

The IOC opened the modern pentathlon to women for the first time at the 2000 games in Sydney, Australia. Stephanie Cook of Great Britain passed Emily deRiel of the United States during the last lap of the 3-k run to win the gold medal. Kate Allenby of Britain won the bronze. Silver medalist deRiel was the first American since Robert Beck (bronze, 1960) to win a medal in the modern pentathlon.

ROWING

Competitive rowing involves the use of oars to propel a shell through water. Rowing events fall into two categories: sculling, in which each rower has two oars, and sweeping oar, in which each rower has only one oar.

Origin of the Sport

Rowing has been around for thousands of years. The ancient Greeks and Romans used slaves and prisoners of war chained below decks to power their warships. The social status of rowers began to improve in the first millennium, when ferrymen began transporting royal barges and the Vikings made their voyages of exploration.

Rowing competitions followed, as races became part of local fairs and celebrations. The first rowing race was held in Venice, Italy, in 1315. One of the oldest sporting events in the world began in 1716, when an English actor named Thomas Doggett offered prize money to the winner of a 4.5-mile (7.8-kilometer) race on the Thames between the London and Chelsea Bridges. This event, known as the Doggett Coat and Badge, still runs annually.

Formal rowing races became hugely popular in England during the 1800s. University students from Oxford and Cambridge began competing against each other in 1829. The most famous rowing race of all, the Henley Royal Regatta, was held for the first time on the Thames River in 1839. By that time, Americans had also taken up the sport. Major races were held in New York Harbor and on the Hudson River. In 1852, students at Yale and Harvard began their own version of the Oxford-Cambridge rivalry. Rowers from Yale and Harvard still compete over a 4-mile (6.4-km) course in Gale's Ferry, Connecticut, in what is the oldest intercollegiate sporting event in the United States.

Competing in the Event

Olympic rowers compete in both sculls and sweeps. Every boat, or shell, in a sweep event has an equal number of oars: one on the left side, the next on the right side, and so on. An

Fast Facts

First Olympic competition

Paris, France; 1900

Legendary athletes

Jack Kelly, **USA**

Elisabeta Lipa, **Romania**

Steven Redgrave,
Great Britain

Criteria for winning

First across the finish line

extra person, called a coxswain (pronounced *cox'n*) sits at the rear of the shell for some sweep events. The coxswain faces the rowers, shouts instructions to the crew, and uses a rudder to steer. Because they do not row, coxswains are generally small and light, adding as little weight as possible. Although coxed pairs and fours crews (those with a coxswain) have rowed in previous Olympic competitions, only coxless pairs and fours crews (those without a coxswain) now compete in the Olympics. All eights carry a coxswain.

Shells are made of strong, lightweight materials such as Kevlar, which also is used to make bulletproof vests. Shells are long and sleek, designed to glide smoothly through the water. They are also narrow—only 10 inches (25.4 centimeters) wide for singles and 20 inches (50.8 cm) wide for the larger boats. Boats range in weight and length from about 30 pounds (13.6 kilograms) and 27 feet (8.2 m) long for a single shell, to 205 lb (93.1 kg) and 60 ft (18.3 m) long for an eight-person shell.

Competitive rowers face the rear of the shell. Their oars are attached to the sides of the boat. Shells have seats that slide back and forth, enabling the rower to use his or her leg muscles—the body's strongest muscle group—to power the boat. The rower's feet rest on a plate, mounted at an angle, at the bottom of the shell. On each stroke, the rower pulls the oar through the water while pushing back with his or

Competitive rowing requires enormous upper and lower body strength. The Australian women (in green) row to victory in the double sculls event at the 1996 games in Atlanta.

her legs. As the rower's legs straighten, the seat slides backward. All of this pulling and pushing helps the rower generate power. It also helps make rowers some of the fittest athletes in the world.

The course is 2,000 meters long and divided into six lanes. Each lane is 13.5 m (44 ft) wide. The water must be at least 3.5 m (11.5 ft) deep. Rowers advance through preliminary heats. The crews with the six fastest times meet in the final round.

In the Olympics

Rowing has been an official medal sport for men at the Summer Olympics since 1900. In 1976, the IOC added events for women. Olympic rowing consists of eight events for men and six for women. All are in the open class, which means that rowers can be any weight. In 1996, lightweight events were included in the Olympics for the first time. Rowing is one of the last truly amateur sports in the Olympics. The eight-man team from East Germany that won the gold medal at the 1976 Olympics, for instance, included a butcher, a plumber, a gardener, a mechanic, and a student.

German athletes have dominated Olympic rowing since 1900, winning 107 Olympic medals. Frank Forberger, Frank Ruhle, Dieter Grahn, and Dieter Schubert of East Germany were an unbeaten foursome in 11 years of international competition. They were the Olympic coxless four gold medalists in 1968 and 1972. Twin brothers Bernd and Jorg Landvoigt of East Germany won an Olympic bronze medal in eights in 1972.

Thanks to its collegiate rowing tradition, the United States has done well in men's eights competition. American crews have won ten Olympic gold medals, including eight consecutive medals between 1900 and 1960. One member of the 1924 U.S. eight-man crew was a Yale University student named Benjamin Spock, who later became a world-famous doctor and expert on raising healthy babies.

Jack Kelly, who once won 126 consecutive races, was the greatest American sculler of all time. His major victories were Olympic gold medals in singles and doubles in 1920 and 1924. His son, John Kelly Jr., was an Olympic bronze

MYSTERY BOY

The youngest competitor in modern Olympic history was a coxswain who helped the two-man crew from Holland to win the gold medal in Paris, France, in 1900. The French boy, whose name is not known, may have been as young as seven years old.

medalist in singles in 1956. His daughter, Grace, was a famous movie actress who later became Princess of Monaco.

Five rowers have won gold medals in three different Olympiads: Paul Costello of the United States (1920–1928), Jack Beresford of Great Britain (1924–1936), Vyacheslav Ivanov of the Soviet Union (1956–1964), Siegfried Brietzke of East Germany (1972–1980), and Pertti Karppinen of Finland (1976–1984). British rower Steven Redgrave has the distinction of winning gold medals in five Olympic Games. Redgrave won the four-man shell with coxswain in 1984 (since discontinued), the two-man shell in 1988 (paired with Andrew Holmes), and the two-man shell again in 1992 and 1996 (paired with Matthew Pinsent). In 2000, Redgrave won the coxless four for an unprecedented fifth gold medal.

Italian brothers Giuseppe and Carmine Abbagnale won a record nine world championships in coxed pairs between 1981 and 1991. They also won Olympic gold medals in 1984 and 1988. Another Abbagnale brother, Agostino, won the gold in the quadruple sculls in 1988. At the 1992 Olympics, Australia won its first gold medal in the coxless four sweep event. The four Aussie rowers became known as the Oarsome Foursome.

Romania and Canada have dominated the women's rowing events. In 1984, Romanian women stroked to five gold medals and one silver in their six races. Olga Homeghi-Bularda and Rodica Puscatu-Arba each won four Olympic medals. They later teamed up to win 40 straight races between 1986 and 1988 in coxless pair. Their streak was topped off with a gold medal in coxless pair and a silver in the eights at the 1988 Olympics. In 1996, Romania's Elisabeta Lipa became the first rower in Olympic history to win six medals (three gold, two silver, and one bronze).

Canadian women medaled in four of six events in 1992 and again in 1996. The two-woman team of Marnie McBean and Kathleen Heddle became the first Canadians in any sport to win three gold medals. The most outstanding Canadian single rower is Silken Laumann. When her shell was struck by another boat before the 1992 Olympics, a severe leg injury threatened to put an end to her rowing career. In Barcelona, Laumann, who had recovered from her injury, came back to win a bronze medal in single sculls.

SAILING

In sailing, the shortest distance between two points is a "Z." This refers to the zigzag pattern, called tacking, that sailors use to travel upwind (opposite to the direction in which the wind is blowing). Tacking and modern sail design are key elements in competitive sailing events.

Origin of the Sport

People have been boating for recreation and travel since ancient times. Pleasure sailing was popular among the aristocracy in Europe, especially in Holland, in the early 1600s. As the Dutch colonized parts of the Americas, southern Africa, and the East Indies, they developed fast and agile sailing vessels to protect their cargoes. The sport of sailing spread to England, and the first sailing club was established in Cork, Ireland, in 1720. Yachting eventually came to the Americas, and the first American association—the Knickerbocker Boat Club—formed on Long Island in 1811.

In 1906, the International Yacht Racing Union established the rule that became the standard for the 1908 games, the first Olympiad to include sailing events. After the 1920 games in Antwerp, Belgium, the IOC adopted "one-design" classifications. Each boat in a class is built from the same design, with strict guidelines to ensure that it is virtually identical to the others.

Competing in the Event

The yachting competition at the Summer Games includes races for nine types of boats: Europe, Finn, 470, 49er, Laser, Soling, Star, Tornado, and Mistral (or Sailboard). A single person sails the boats in the Europe, Finn, Laser, and Sailboard classes. The large sail on the Finn makes it an especially challenging boat to sail.

Two-person crews compete in the 470, 49er, Star, and Tornado classes. Three people crew the Soling event. The boats range in size from the 11-foot (3.3-meter) Europe to the 26-ft (7.9-m) Soling. A Sailboard, as its name implies, is much like a surfboard with a sail attached.

Fast Facts

First Olympic competition

London, England; 1908

Legendary athletes

Paul Elvstrom, **Denmark**

Valentyn Mankin, **Soviet Union**

Criteria for winning

Lowest score

The two-person team from Japan is shown here in the 470 class competition at the 1996 games in Atlanta.

There are 11 Olympic sailing events. Men and women compete in the 470 and Sailboard classes in separate races. The Finn is for men only, and the Europe is for women only. Men and women compete against each other in the five other classes (Soling, Star, Tornado, Laser, and 49er).

All boats in any given race are of the same design, thereby testing the skills of the crew rather than features of the boat. Boats sail a course consisting of several segments, or legs, and marked by buoys. The boat must round the buoys in sequence, although the skipper determines the route. The average course is about 11 miles (17.7 kilometers); faster boats run the longer courses.

Olympic sailing events are a series of races. Scoring is based on a low-point system. Boats receive points for the order in which they finish, with the winner receiving one point. The series winner is the boat that has the lowest score. A new set of scoring rules, introduced in 2000, made it possible for each boat to drop its two worst (or highest) scores after nine races. The scores for the last race in each class may not be dropped.

In the Olympics

The United States has won the most medals overall in Olympic sailing history, with a total of 54. In 1992, the American team claimed nine medals in ten classes.

Paul Elvstrom of Denmark has won the most individual gold medals in Olympic yachting. In 1948, he won his first of four consecutive gold medals, competing solo in the Firefly class. Elvstrom returned to the games in 1952 to compete in the Finn class, capturing his second gold medal. His third and fourth came in 1956 and 1960, respectively.

Valentyn Mankin of the Soviet Union, another championship sailor, is the only yachtsman to have won gold medals in three different classes. He won the gold in the Finn class in 1968, gold in the Tempest class (discontinued after 1976) in 1972, and gold in the Star class in 1980. He also won a silver medal in the Tempest class in 1976.

SHOOTING

Most Olympic athletes need either strength or speed to compete in their sports. Shooters, on the other hand, need a calm disposition and a steady hand and arm. Shooting is a sport of marksmanship—the skill of hitting a target, or mark.

Origin of the Sport

Shooting competitions have existed since the 1300s—around the same time that firearms were invented. The first recorded shooting contest occurred in 1477 in Eichstadt, Germany. Contestants used the blunderbuss—a gun with a short barrel and a flared muzzle to facilitate loading the weapon with gunpowder.

Pistols, first associated with the practice of dueling, eventually replaced swords in the 1700s. In the 1800s, exhibition shooting at circuses and fairs led to a greater focus on accuracy and skill. "Buffalo Bill" Cody and Annie Oakley were probably the most famous exhibition shooters, and they deserve credit for promoting the sport.

Trap shooting did not originate in the American West, but it was wild! It was based on an English sport called high hats, in which live birds were placed under the shooters' hats. When the signal was given, the shooter lifted his hat and the bird took off. The shooter could not shoot at the bird until his hat was back on his head, thus giving the bird a "flying start."

Competing in the Event

There are currently 17 shooting events in the Olympics. Men and women use air- or gas-powered pistols to fire lead pellets at targets 10 meters (32.8 feet) away. The target has a bull's-eye that is smaller than a dime. In some pistol events, such as the free pistol, shooters have 2 hours and 30 minutes to fire 60 shots. In other events, such as the rapid-fire pistol, shooters must fire in rapid succession.

Because rifles are generally more accurate than pistols, the targets used in rifle competitions are smaller than those used in pistol shooting. In the air rifle event, for example, the bull's-eye is 1 millimeter in diameter—about the size of

Fast Facts

First Olympic competition

Athens, Greece; 1896

Legendary athletes

Jasna Sekaric, **Yugoslavia**
Ragnar Skanakar, **Sweden**
Lones Wigger, **USA**

Criteria for winning

Highest score

In the pistol events, athletes aim for a bull's-eye that is smaller than a dime.

a pencil point! In the air rifle event, men and women use air- or gas-powered rifles to fire lead pellets at a target 10 m (32.8 ft) away. Men have 1 hour and 45 minutes for 60 shots. Women have 1 hour and 15 minutes for 40 shots.

In the three-position rifle event, men and women fire from prone (lying down), standing, and kneeling positions. The target, which is 50 m (164 ft) away, has a bull's-eye that is smaller than a dime. Men fire 40 shots from each position, for a total of 120 shots, with a perfect score of 1,200. The time limit is 1 hour for prone, 1 hour and 30 minutes for the standing stage, and 1 hour and 15 minutes for the kneeling stage. Women fire 20 shots in each position (60 shots total), with 600 as a perfect score. They have a total of 2 hours and 30 minutes to shoot from all positions.

An Olympic competition for men since 1900, the moving target event is the only shooting contest that allows the use of a telescopic sight. Shooters use air- or gas-powered rifles to fire pellets at targets moving along a track 10 m (32.8 ft) away. The target has two bull's-eyes placed 6 inches (15 cm) apart, each the size of a pencil eraser. The match consists of 60 shots, divided into 30 slow runs and 30 fast runs. During slow runs, a shooter has 5 seconds to fire at the moving targets. During fast runs, the target appears for only 2.5 seconds.

There are three Olympic shotgun events—skeet, trap, and double trap. Trap shooting has been an Olympic event for men since 1900. In this contest, shooters fire a shotgun from five different shooting stations. The target is a 4-inch

(10-cm) clay disk called a clay pigeon. It is hidden in an underground bunker called a trap house. Each trap house contains a device that flings the "pigeon" into the air.

When the shooter is ready, he or she yells "Pull!" and a disk is fired from the trap house at a speed of up to 65 miles (105 km) per hour. The shooter is allowed two shots at each target. The match consists of 125 targets, and 125 is a perfect score.

Skeet shooting was added to the Olympics in 1968. Like trap shooting, competitors fire shotguns at clay pigeons. In skeet, however, competitors shoot from eight stations at targets coming from two trap houses. Clay pigeons are released either from the high trap house, which is 10 ft (3 m) off the ground, or from the low trap house, which is 3 ft (0.9 m) off the ground. Sometimes two clay pigeons are released at the same time. Competitors may fire one shot at each of 125 targets.

Men and women have competed in the double-trap event since the 1996 Olympics in Atlanta. In double trap, competitors fire shotguns from five different stations. At each station, clay pigeons are hurled two at a time from an underground trap house at speeds of up to 50 miles (80 km) per hour. The goal is to hit both clay targets.

In the Olympics

Shooting was one of nine sports at the first modern Olympics in 1896. Shooting has always been a strong Olympic sport for the United States. U.S. athletes have won 69 individual medals, including 30 gold.

Swedish gunmaker Ragnar Skanakar won four Olympic medals in free pistol during a 20-year span—gold in 1972, silver in 1984 and 1988, and bronze in 1992. Another star shooter was Lones Wigger of the United States, who won a gold medal in three-position rifle in 1964 (this set a new world record) and in free rifle in 1972, and a silver medal in free-rifle prone in 1964.

Jasna Sekaric is Yugoslavia's most successful female athlete. In 1988, she won the gold medal in air pistol and the bronze medal in sport pistol. In 1992, she captured the silver medal in air pistol.

SINGLE-HANDED

Winning a gold medal in rapid-fire in 1948 and again in 1952, Károly Tákacs of Hungary is one of only five competitors to successfully defend his Olympic shooting title. What is more remarkable is that he did it left-handed. In 1938, while he was serving in the army, a grenade exploded in his right hand—his shooting hand. Tákacs taught himself to shoot with his left hand.

SOCCER

Soccer is called football in every country of the world except the United States and Canada. Without using their hands, players dribble and pass the ball down the field and kick or head-butt the ball into the opponent's goal. Only the goalie can use his or her hands to stop the ball.

Origin of the Sport

Soccer began nearly 4,000 years ago in China. The Greeks and Romans also had versions of the game. By the 1100s, kicking games were popular in Britain. Played by huge groups of people, sometimes over miles of countryside, the sport had no real rules. These games could become so rough that they became a danger to passersby. Because of this, King Edward II outlawed them in 1314.

Modern soccer began in the early 1800s, when it was introduced in England's schools. In 1862, J.C. Thring created rules for what he called "The Simplest Game," and the following year, the London Football Association (LFA) was formed. In 1871, the LFA held its first championship, which was open to all amateur soccer clubs. During the late 1800s, soccer spread throughout the world. British sailors played the game wherever their ships docked. In 1904, the Federation Internationale des Football Associations (FIFA) was formed. FIFA is the organization that governs the sport today.

Competing in the Event

Soccer is played by two teams of 11 players each. The object is to score goals, each worth one point. Soccer games are 90 minutes long, with two 45-minute halves. The referee on the field keeps the time, and time-outs are called only for an injured player. Each team may make only two substitutions during the game. After a player has left the game, he or she cannot return. Players who are in for the entire game may run as many as 10 miles.

In addition to the goalie, a team has defenders, midfielders, and forwards. The defenders are the last line of defense

Fast Facts

First Olympic competition

Paris, France; 1900

Legendary athletes

Mia Hamm, USA
Sophus Nielsen, Denmark

Criteria for winning

Most goals scored

in front of the goalkeeper. By breaking up a play, they can prevent the opponent from scoring. The midfielders link the offense and the defense. The forwards' main job is to score by driving the ball past the other team's defense and into the net. Players may move the ball down the field using their head, chest, legs, and feet. The only time a player other than the goalie is allowed to use his or her hands is on a throw-in, which occurs after the ball has gone out of bounds.

Olympic soccer is played on a field about 105 meters (344 feet) long and 64 m (210 ft) wide, which is slightly larger than an American football field. The goals are centered at either end of the field.

When a team commits a violation, such as an offside, the other team gets a free kick. When a player commits a major foul within his or her team's penalty area, the other team is allowed a penalty kick.

Referees may issue warnings in the form of yellow or red cards. A yellow card means that a player has committed a serious foul, such as tripping an opponent. After two yellow cards, a player is thrown out of the game. A player who commits a very serious foul, such as tackling from behind, is shown a red card and is immediately kicked out of the game.

In the Olympics

Soccer was the first team sport played at the Olympics. Great Britain dominated the early competitions, winning three of the first four tournaments (1900–1912). The 1908 Danish team was led by Sophus Nielsen, who set an international soccer record by scoring ten goals in an early-round game against France. Nielsen still holds the record for most goals in Olympic competition, 13. Even so, Great Britain defeated Denmark in the finals.

At the 1920 games in Antwerp, Belgium, the final match pitted the home team against a powerful team from Czechoslovakia, which had outscored its opponents 15-1 on its way to the final. After the Belgian team streaked out to a 2-0 lead late in the first half, the referee ejected Czech star Karel Steiner for rough play. When the entire Czech squad walked off the field in protest, the players were disqualified and the gold medal went to the Belgian team.

TOO MANY STAR PLAYERS

A new rule, adopted in 1992, set an age limit of 23 for Olympic soccer players. Although each team is allowed three exceptions (called wild-card players), the ruling helps to limit the number of World Cup stars who play in the Olympic Games.

The introduction of the World Cup soccer tournament weakened the stature of Olympic soccer, and the sport was excluded from the 1932 games in Los Angeles. When the sport returned to the Olympic program in 1936 in Berlin, the Italian team, led by Annibale Frossi, defeated Austria for the gold medal.

By 1948, Eastern European teams dominated Olympic soccer. At the 1948 Olympic Games in London, Sweden beat Yugoslavia for the gold. Sweden was the last noncommunist team to win an Olympic soccer tournament until 1992.

Yugoslavia, the second-place finisher in 1948, 1952, and 1956, finally won the gold medal at the 1960 Olympiad in Rome. The Yugoslavs defeated Denmark in the final match, even though their team captain had been expelled from the game for insulting a referee. Hungary won two consecutive gold medals, beating Czechoslovakia in 1964 and Bulgaria in 1968. The referee had ejected three Bulgarian players, forcing the team to play the second half with only eight players.

Rule changes in 1984 allowed professional soccer players to compete in the Olympics for the first time. France won the final match against Brazil on two second-half goals. In 1988, the United States made it to the quarterfinals, but then lost to the Soviet Union, whose team made it to first place. The Soviet Union had outscored Brazil, 2-1, in overtime. Brazil has won the World Cup four times, more than any other nation, but has never captured the Olympic gold.

Playing before the hometown fans in Barcelona, Spain won its first-ever Olympic soccer gold in 1992. The pre-Olympic favorites at the 1996 games in Atlanta were Brazil and Argentina. Both teams reached the semifinals, but Nigeria upset Brazil and then went on to a stunning victory over Argentina in the final. At the 2000 Olympic soccer final, Cameroon, which had never won a medal, defeated Spain. The U.S. men had an impressive tournament, beating Japan in the quarterfinal round to go further than any American men's soccer team had ever gone in the Summer Games. The Americans lost to Chile in the bronze-medal match, however. The American men still have not won an Olympic medal.

Women's soccer was added to the Olympic program in 1996, and the U.S. women's team claimed the first gold medal. American Mia Hamm, perhaps the best female player in the world, sat out the first round with an injured ankle. She was back for the semifinal match against Norway, which was a thriller of a game. In sudden-death overtime, American midfielder Shannon MacMillan scored the winning goal in the 100th minute. The United States faced China for the championship. Hamm set up both goals, and the United States won 2-1.

The American women were back in 2000 to try to defend their gold medal. The squad returned with 14 of the 18 players who had won the 1999 World Cup. In the semifinal game against Brazil, Hamm scored a goal in the second half to give the Americans a 1-0 victory and a place in the gold-medal game against Norway. This match will be remembered as one of the greatest women's games ever played. Norway was leading 2-1 late in the second half and was determined to hold off an American rally. The United States forced the game into overtime when Tiffeny Milbrett headed a brilliant cross from Mia Hamm into the net less than a minute from the end of regulation play. Although the momentum had swung to the Americans, Norway rebounded to defeat the United States 3-2 for the gold medal.

Spain's Roberto Solozabal (right) and Ghana's Yaw Preko go for the ball during a match at the 1992 Olympics. Spain triumphed over Ghana 2-0, then went on to defeat Poland for the gold at the Barcelona games.

SOFTBALL

Softball is played like baseball; the rules are essentially the same. There are, however, several important differences. These include pitching style, type and size of ball, distance between pitcher and batter, number of innings, and handling of scoring ties.

Origin of the Sport

On Thanksgiving Day in 1887, while awaiting the final score of the Yale-Harvard football game, George Hancock and 20 or so young men invented softball inside the Farragut Boat Club in Chicago. A man tossed a boxing glove to another man, who whacked the glove back to the pitcher with a pole. That gave Hancock an idea. He tied the laces of the boxing glove together to form a ball and marked off a baseball diamond on the gym floor, and the men played a game of "indoor baseball." Hancock later drew up a set of rules, and the Farragut team soon challenged other gyms to games. The sport became immensely popular and soon moved outdoors.

Softball gradually spread throughout the United States. In 1895, Lewis Rober, head of the Minneapolis fire department, decided the game would help keep his firemen fit. Soon other fire companies caught softball fever. Leagues formed, and crowds of enthusiastic fans attended the games. The game continued to spread to the Midwest and eventually to the rest of the country. In the late 1920s, the Amateur Softball Association (ASA) was formed to regulate and promote the sport. From two national championships in the 1930s, the ASA has expanded to more than 60 championship events for men, women, and coed teams.

Competing in the Event

In some respects, softball is a miniature version of baseball. In softball, the pitcher's mound is 40 feet (12.2 meters) from home plate instead of 60.5 ft (18.4 m), as in baseball. The bases are 60 ft (18 m) apart instead of 90 ft (27.4 m). The outfield fence is about 200 ft (60.9 m) from home plate in center field instead of 400 ft (121.8 m). Softball games

Fast Facts

First Olympic competition

Atlanta, Georgia; 1996

Legendary athletes

Lisa Fernandez, USA
Dot Richardson, USA

Criteria for winning

Most runs scored

last seven innings instead of nine. The only part of softball that is not a miniature version of baseball is the ball itself, which is 12 inches (30.5 centimeters) in circumference. A baseball is 9 inches (22.8 cm) in circumference.

As in baseball, each softball team fields nine players: pitcher, catcher, first baseman, second baseman, third baseman, shortstop, left fielder, center fielder, and right fielder. Softball consists of seven innings, with three outs in each. In the event of a tie, the game continues until one team has scored more runs by the end of a completed inning. If the score is still tied after nine innings, each team begins its half of the inning with a runner on second base.

Unlike baseball pitchers, softball pitchers throw underhand. The best fast-pitch softball pitchers throw the ball straight, and often as hard as a major-league fastball. They also try to fool batters by throwing pitches that rise, drop, or curve. During the windup, the pitcher is allowed one step forward in the direction of the batter. Pitchers dominate to such an extent that typical game scores are low and home runs are rare. The team at bat tries to move its runners around the bases with a string of singles and doubles. As in baseball, bunts and stolen bases are common. Unlike baseball, the softball player may not leave the base until the ball is pitched.

In the Olympics

Fast-pitch softball became an Olympic sport at the 1996 games in Atlanta, Georgia. Only women compete in the event. Eight teams participate—the host country, the three winners of the regional qualifying tournaments, and the four semifinalists of the most recent world championship. In 1996, the United States, with its 106-game winning streak begun in 1986, was favored to win the gold medal. At the Olympics, the Americans won their first five games in the preliminary round and then faced Australia. In the fifth inning, third baseman Dani Tyler smacked a home run that should have given the United States a 1-0 lead. In her excitement to high-five her jubilant teammates, however, Tyler failed to touch home plate. The Australians realized the mistake and tagged her out. The blunder ultimately lost the game for the United States.

UNEXPECTED BOOST

Ironically, the Great Depression of the early 1930s boosted the popularity of softball. First of all, thousands of unemployed people had time to play. In addition, as part of President Franklin Roosevelt's New Deal program, more than 3,000 athletic fields were built in the United States during that time. Many of the fields had lights, making them suitable for night games.

American Shelia Douty leaps up to catch the ball as Vilma Alvarez of Cuba runs to the base. The U.S. team beat Cuba 3-0 in this game and went on to win the gold medal at the 2000 games in Sydney.

Meanwhile, American ace pitcher Lisa Fernandez had been throwing a perfect game. The United·States was ahead 1-0 at the top of the tenth inning. Fernandez had retired 29 batters in a row—15 of these had been strikeouts. The Australians had not hit a single ball beyond the infield! With two outs at the bottom of the tenth inning, Fernandez was one strike away from a perfect-game victory. Then her former UCLA teammate, Joanne Brown, came to bat and turned Fernandez's pitch into a home run that tied the score. Because softball rules allowed Australia to start the inning with a runner on second base, two runners came home, and the Australians won 2-1. The United States had been beaten, and Fernandez lost a game in which she had retired all but one batter.

Springing back from defeat, the U.S. squad won two more games before facing China in the gold-medal game. In the bottom of the third inning, with one runner on base, Dot Richardson, a 34-year-old orthopedic surgeon, lined a ball just inside the right field foul pole for a home run and a 2-0 lead. The United States went on to win the game and the gold, 3-1.

The U.S. softball team came to Sydney in 2000 as the defending Olympic champions. They won the opening game, a no-hitter pitched by Lori Harrigan against Canada. In later round-robin play, however, they hit their first ever three-game losing skid in 35 years of international play. The team seemed completely demoralized until Fernandez struck out 25 batters in 12 innings against Australia. Then Fernandez surrendered a decisive two-run home run in the 13th inning to lose a 2-1 heartbreaker.

Following that bitter defeat, the American players gathered in the shower, in uniform, for a "voodoo cleansing" to rid themselves of the losing curse. It must have worked, because they went on to win five consecutive games and to successfully defend their championship by beating Japan in the gold-medal game. The women from the United States triumphed in the eighth inning when a Japanese outfielder dropped a fly ball that enabled the winning run to score. It was the team's second straight gold medal.

SWIMMING

Swimming has existed since the first human faced a body of water that blocked his or her way. Today, competitive swimmers use four strokes—freestyle, backstroke, butterfly, and breaststroke—to win races and to set new speed records.

Origin of the Sport

Swimming has been popular throughout history. The Greek historians Herodotus and Thucydides wrote about the sport in the 400s B.C. The Greek traveler and geographer Pausanias, who wrote about local history and customs of the places he visited, described swimming races held to honor the god Dionysis. During the late Middle Ages, books on swimming were published throughout Europe. An edict by the emperor of Japan in 1603 made swimming a part of the school curriculum, which eventually led to organized competitions among students. Regular swimming events began to develop in Europe in the 1800s. By 1837, London had six swimming pools that were used for aquatic contests.

Swimming as a competitive sport developed more slowly in North America. The Dolphin Swim Club in Toronto, Canada, formed in 1876. The first major race in the United States occurred in 1883. Sponsored by the New York Athletic Club, the event was billed as a national championship. Toward the end of the 1800s, the distinction between amateurs and professionals became a major issue in many competitive sports. Following the formation of the Amateur Swimming Association in 1886, swimming instructors were excluded from racing.

Swimming contests have been part of the Olympics since the first modern Olympiad in 1896. Immediately following the London games in 1908, representatives from eight European nations met to form the Fédération Internationale de Natation Amateur (FINA). FINA's primary tasks were to establish rules for swimming events, to verify and monitor world records, and to organize programs for the Olympic Games. FINA lobbied for the inclusion of swimming events for women, which occurred at the 1912 games in Stockholm, Sweden.

Fast Facts

First Olympic competition

Athens, Greece; 1896

Legendary athletes

Kornelia Ender, **East Germany**
Kristin Otto, **East Germany**
Mark Spitz, **USA**
Johnny Weissmuller, **USA**

Criteria for winning

Fastest time

FROM POOL TO JUNGLE

When Johnny Weiss-muller's swimming career ended, he starred in several Tarzan movies. When he became too old to play Tarzan, another Olympic swimmer, Buster Crabbe (400-m freestyle champion of 1932), took over the role.

Competing in the Event

Olympic swimmers compete in 32 events—16 for men and 16 for women. Athletes swim races of various distances in freestyle, backstroke, breaststroke, butterfly, individual medley (in which swimmers use all four strokes), and team relays. Although freestyle swimmers are free to choose any stroke they want, they always use the crawl because it is the fastest stroke. Freestyle swimmers, facedown in the water, move their arms overhead one at a time. To breathe, they turn their head to the side every few strokes. Freestylers use a flutter kick, moving their legs up and down like scissors. The backstroke is an upside-down version of the crawl. On their backs in the water, backstrokers lift their arms overhead one at a time to pull themselves along. They also use a flutter kick, but they can take a breath whenever they need to because their faces are out of the water.

The breaststroke, one of the oldest swimming strokes, is the slowest and most relaxed competitive stroke. Even so, it is difficult to master. The swimmer floats on his or her stomach, with the legs slightly bent. The swimmer's arms begin outstretched, with the hands almost touching, and push outward from each other in a circular motion. Arms may not come out of the water. At the same time, the knees are brought toward the chest and then kicked outward in froglike fashion. During a cycle of one arm stroke and one leg kick, the swimmer's head breaks the surface of the water for a breath.

The newest swimming stroke, the butterfly, is both the most beautiful and the most physically demanding stroke. It developed in the 1930s, when breaststrokers discovered they could swim faster if they lifted their arms out of the water at the end of each stroke to recover for the next stroke. To begin the butterfly, swimmers lie facedown in the water with their arms straight ahead, as in the breaststroke. The swimmer pulls the arms outward, then deeper into the water, and then back toward his or her legs. At the end of the stroke, the swimmer's arms come out of the water and are thrown forward to the starting position. The arms look like butterfly wings as they swing forward above the water. As the arms come out of the water, the swimmer lifts his or her head for a breath. The dolphin kick is used to help propel the swimmer along in the butterfly.

Olympic freestyle swimmers compete in 50-, 100-, 200-, and 400-meter races. Women also swim an 800-m race, and men swim a 1,500-m. Backstroke, breaststroke, and butterfly are contested at both 100 and 200 meters. In the individual medley, the swimmer completes 50 or 100 meters in each of the four strokes, usually in the following order: butterfly, backstroke, breaststroke, and freestyle. In a relay competition, four members of each team swim the same distance in succession. In a medley relay, each swimmer swims the same distance but with a different stroke. One swimmer "hands off" to the next swimmer by touching the wall of the pool.

An Olympic swimming pool is divided into a minimum of eight lanes, each of which is 7 to 9 feet wide. The lanes keep the swimmers apart while they are racing. Plastic markers, called lane lines, run the length of the pool. In addition to organizing the pool into lanes, the lane lines absorb the waves that the swimmers create. At the end of each lane is a touch pad that electronically measures a swimmer's time to a hundredth of a second.

Because there are so many competitors in Olympic swimming, qualifying heats are held. The winners of the heats go on to a final race. The swimmers with the fastest qualifying times swim in the centermost lanes, which have a slight advantage because there may be less water turbulence, and the slowest swimmers use the outside lanes. At the sound of

American Matt Biondi won the silver medal in the 100-meter butterfly, losing to Suriname's Anthony Neste by one hundredth of a second at the 1988 games.

the starting gun, swimmers in freestyle, breaststroke, and butterfly events dive off raised starting platforms into the water. For the backstroke, swimmers start in the water and push off the wall when the gun sounds. In an Olympic pool, every race longer than 50 m requires the swimmer to make a turn in order to swim back the other way. Quick turns can make the difference between first place and last place. Freestyle and backstroke swimmers use a flip turn—an underwater somersault—to reverse direction. Butterfly and breaststroke swimmers use an open turn, keeping their heads above water while reversing direction.

The sprint races (50-m and 100-m) require an all-out effort from start to finish. The 200-m race is a controlled sprint, or almost full speed. For the longer distances (400-, 800-, and 1,500-m races), swimmers pace themselves in order to have the energy for a final all-out sprint at the end of the race. Because every fraction of a second counts in swimming, competitors wear skintight suits made of slick materials and swim caps to reduce resistance. Some even shave their bodies. The only equipment swimmers use is a pair of goggles, which enable them to keep their eyes open while speeding through the water.

In the Olympics

Olympic swimming has undergone many changes since the first modern Olympiad in 1896. For starters, those early competitions took place in a bay near Piraeus, Greece. Swimmers started each of the three races by diving from boats. The water temperature was only 55 degrees Fahrenheit, and the waves were 12 ft high. Alfréd Hajós of Hungary won the 100-m and the 1,200-m freestyle races. Hajós, who had covered himself with grease to protect himself from the freezing water, later recalled, "My will to live completely overcame my desire to win."

Duke Kahanamoku of Hawaii, the man who popularized surfing as a sport, was a world-class swimmer before taking up surfing. He won gold medals in the 100-m freestyle in 1912 and 1920 and a silver medal in 1924. American Johnny Weissmuller was the first swimmer to break the one-minute barrier in the 100-m freestyle race. At the 1924 games, he won gold medals in the 100-m and 400-m freestyle events. He also took the gold in the 100-m freestyle in 1928.

By 1932, Japan's swimmers had undermined American dominance of the sport. That year, Japanese men won all but one of the men's Olympic swimming events. With Japan absent from the 1948 Olympics because of its role in World War II, however, the United States captured six gold medals, including a sweep of the three freestyle races.

The 1956 Olympic Games in Melbourne belonged to the Australians. Led by Murray Rose, who won the 400-m and 1,500-m freestyle events, the Australian team captured five gold medals.

The Australians swept the three men's individual freestyle events again in 1960. John Devitt won the 100 m, Murray Rose retained his 400-m title, and John Konrads took the gold in the 1,500-m race. Controversy dampened Devitt's victory, however. Poolside judges had declared Devitt the winner, but the electronic timer gave American Lance Larson a faster time. Four years of protest failed to change the result. In 1964, Don Schollander of the United States became the first Olympian to win four gold medals in a single Olympiad. In 1968, the Americans took home ten medals—more than any other country.

Mark Spitz was the undeniable champion of the 1972 games in Munich, capturing four individual races (freestyle sprints and butterfly events) and swimming on three winning relay teams. He won seven gold medals and set world records in each race. Spitz, who had won two gold medals in 1968, as well as a bronze and silver, earned a total of 11 medals in his Olympic career.

Before 1980, the Soviet men had never won a gold medal for swimming. With the United States out of competition that year, however, the Russian men's team captured seven gold, seven silver, and three bronze medals. Vladimir Salnikov led the way with three gold medals. In the 1,500-m freestyle, Salnikov set a new world record, finishing the race in less than 15 minutes.

Among the highlights of the 1988 swimming competition in Seoul, Korea, was West Germany's Michael Gross breaking the world record that had been set four years earlier. Nicknamed the Albatross because of his height (6 feet 7 inches) and tremendous arm span, Gross aced the 200-m

SYNCHRONIZED SWIMMING

Synchronized means "at the same time." In synchronized swimming, teams of two and eight women perform balletic moves to music. Each team performs a 2-minute 50-second technical routine and a 5-minute free program. Moves include spiraling headfirst into the water so that only the swimmer's toes remain above water, or building a pyramid of swimmers. Seven judges score each team on creativity, difficulty of moves, and how well the swimmers on the team are synchronized with one another. American and Canadian women have dominated synchronized swimming since its Olympic debut in 1984. Americans placed fourth at the 2000 Olympics, behind a near-perfect Russian team, Japan, and Canada.

HEADS UP!

Because backstrokers cannot see where they are going, they could easily smash headfirst into the concrete pool wall. To prevent unnecessary headaches, a line of colorful flags is hung across the pool five meters from each end. Swimmers know exactly how many strokes it takes to reach the wall once they pass under the flags.

butterfly 0.10 second faster than the previous record. American Matt Biondi won five gold medals, one silver, and one bronze in Seoul. His total of 11 medals (eight gold, two silver, one bronze) equaled Mark Spitz's career record.

Tamas Darnyi of Hungary won the 200-m and 400-m individual medleys, smashing his own best times in both events. He won both events again at the 1992 games. That same year, Aleksandr Popov of Russia defeated Matt Biondi in the 50-m freestyle and won the 100-m race.

Swimming events for women were added to the Olympic Games in 1912. Australia's Fanny Durack, who held every world record in women's swimming from 50 yards to 1 mile, won the first women's Olympic swimming event, the 100-m freestyle. Durack's toughest challenge had occurred before the games, when she had to convince the Australian team to send a woman to the Olympics.

Ethelda Bleibtrey of the United States won all three women's events at the 1920 games in Antwerp, Belgium. The previous year, Bleibtrey had been arrested for swimming without stockings at New York's Manhattan Beach. Gertrude Ederle, perhaps best known for swimming the English Channel, won bronze medals in the 100-m and 400-m freestyle events and the gold in the freestyle relay in 1924.

Australia's Dawn Fraser, who won a total of four gold medals and four silver medals between 1956 and 1964, was often at the center of controversy. Fraser had frequent arguments with officials, but she also had an enormous amount of talent. She had held the world record for 15 years for the 100-m freestyle. In 1964, she was the first woman to break one minute for the 100-m event. Fraser also was the first Olympic swimmer to win the same event three times.

East German swimmers made a big splash at the 1976 Summer Olympics in Montreal, Canada, winning 11 of 13 events and beginning a long streak of German domination. KORNELIA ENDER of East Germany was only 13 years old when she won three silver medals at the 1972 Olympics in the 200-m medley and both relay events. In Montreal, Ender won four gold medals and one silver. In 1980, the East German women captured 11 of 13 events, setting seven world records and two Olympic records in the process.

With Soviet-bloc nations boycotting the 1984 games in Los Angeles, the U.S. women's team swam away with 12 gold and 7 silver medals. Nancy Hogshead was the big winner, earning four medals, including a gold medal in the 100-meter freestyle that she shared with teammate Carrie Steinseifer. American Tracy Caulkins, who had been disappointed by the U.S. boycott of the games in 1980, claimed three gold medals at the 1984 Olympiad. Another swimmer affected by the boycott was Mary T. Meagher, who was known as Madame Butterfly because she was such a fast and elegant butterfly swimmer. Meagher won three butterfly gold medals in 1984 and captured the 200-m bronze in 1988.

Kristin Otto of East Germany was one of the most versatile swimmers ever. At the 1988 Olympics in Seoul, South Korea, she won six gold medals—a record for a female swimmer. She captured the 50-m and 100-m freestyle, the 100-m backstroke, the 100-m butterfly, freestyle relay, and medley relay. The East German women might have swept the Seoul games if not for triple–gold medalist Janet Evans of the United States. Evans won gold medals in the 400-m and 800-m freestyle races and the 400-m individual medley. At the 1992 Olympics, Evans won a gold medal in the 800-m freestyle and a silver medal in the 400-m freestyle.

For the second time, in consecutive Olympiads, American swimmer Janet Evans captures the gold in the 800-meter freestyle.

American sprinter Amy Van Dyken earned four gold medals at the 1996 games in Atlanta, Georgia. She was part of two winning relay teams and also won the gold in the 50-m freestyle and the 100-m butterfly events to become the first U.S. woman ever to win four gold medals in one Olympiad. Perhaps the real heroine of the games that year was Michelle Smith of Ireland, who won her country's first swimming medals—three gold medals and a bronze. Jenny Thompson made history as a member of the U.S. relay team that won all three of the women's relay events. The victories gave Thompson eight Olympic gold medals, the most won by an American woman in any Olympic sport.

TABLE TENNIS

Played by millions of people in over 160 countries, table tennis is the world's most popular racket sport. Once a quiet parlor game for the English upper classes, table tennis at the Olympic level is a very physical game. Players need great hand-eye coordination to return a ball that often travels at more than 100 miles (161 kilometers) per hour across the net.

Fast Facts

First Olympic competition

Seoul, South Korea; 1988

Legendary athletes

Chen Jing, **Taiwan**

Jan-Ove Waldner, **Sweden**

Criteria for winning

First to score 21 points

Origin of the Sport

In the 1890s, the American toy company Parker Brothers began manufacturing a game called Indoor Tennis. It became a hit in England, where it was known as Ping-Pong because of the sound the ball made when it hit the racket (ping) and the table (pong). In 1922, three British Ping-Pong players created a set of rules and changed the name of the game to table tennis.

In 1926, table tennis enthusiasts from nine countries met in Berlin, Germany, to found the International Table Tennis Federation (ITTF).

Table tennis today is very different from the game that was played in the 1930s, when championship games could last for several hours. The average competitive match now lasts about 30 minutes.

Competing in the Event

Men's and women's singles and doubles table tennis became official Olympic sports in 1988. Olympic table tennis is played on a wooden table that is 9 feet (2.7 meters) long and 5 ft (1.5 m) wide. The net is 6 inches (15.2 centimeters) high, and the top of the table is 2.5 ft (76 cm) above the ground. The white ball, made of celluloid or a similar plastic, is about 1.5 inches (3.8 cm) in diameter and weighs about 2.5 grams (less than an ounce). It is hit with a paddle that can be any size, shape, or weight, but the part that hits the ball—the blade—must be hard and flat.

Play begins with the serve. The player holds the ball in his or her hand, and then hits it as it falls so that it bounces first on his or her side of the table and then on the other side. If the ball brushes the net on a serve, a let is called and the point is restarted. During a rally, players must return the ball before it bounces twice.

Each player serves five points, and then the other player serves. The first player to reach 21 points, with a margin of two or more points, wins. If the game is tied at 20, the players alternate serves after each point. Singles players must win three out of five games; doubles players must win two out of three.

In the Olympics

China has dominated table tennis since 1988, when it became an Olympic event. China's overall total of 26 medals far outpaces the next-best country, South Korea, which has won 10 medals.

Sweden has claimed two medals in Olympic competition. Jan-Ove Waldner won a gold medal in 1992 and a silver medal in 2000, losing to China's Linghui Kong.

Nan Wang of China beat her doubles partner, Ju Li, in five games to win the women's singles gold medal at the Sydney games. The two joined forces to beat their teammates Sun Jin and Yang Ying for the women's doubles gold. In singles, Chen Jing of Taiwan won the bronze medal. Chen had won the Olympic singles title for China in 1988 and the silver for Taiwan in 1996.

Nan Wang of China sends the ball over the net at the 2000 games in Sydney. She won the gold in the women's singles competition and again, with teammate Yang Ying, in the doubles competition.

TAEKWONDO

Taekwondo involves kicking and striking. *Tae* means "to kick with the foot," *kwon* means "to hit with the fist," and *do* means "the art or way of." It is one of several martial arts that are used for combat and self-defense and practiced as a sport.

Origin of the Sport

Taekwondo has its origins in ancient Korea. It may have developed as an offshoot of Japanese karate or as a form of ancient Chinese boxing. Although the traditions and techniques of this martial art had been practiced for centuries, taekwondo experienced a huge revival in the 1950s. It became part of mandatory military training for Korean soldiers and came to the attention of U.S. soldiers during the Korean War. The martial art spread quickly through the United States. Within the next ten years, countries around the world were holding demonstrations to teach the sport to military personnel and civilians alike. By 1973, the government of Korea had recognized the World Taekwondo Federation (WTF) as the legitimate authority for setting international standards and awarding world titles. The first taekwondo world championship was held in Seoul, Korea, in 1973. The IOC included taekwondo as a demonstration sport at the 1988 and 1992 Olympics.

Competing in the Event

Taekwondo consists of kicks, strikes, stances, and blocks. It uses quick movements, as in karate, and flowing movements, as in tai chi chuan (a Chinese martial art). Competitors engage in three 3-minute rounds, with 1-minute rests between each round. A competitor wins by knocking down an opponent for ten seconds or by scoring the most points. Points are accumulated by delivering strikes (hits) to specific areas on the opponent's body—head, abdomen, and both sides of the body.

Participants wear uniforms called *dobuks* and protective gear on which the scoring areas are marked. Hits below the waist are not allowed. Strikes must be made with the foot

Fast Facts

First Olympic competition

Sydney, Australia; 2000

Legendary athlete

Steven Lopez, USA

Criteria for winning

Knockdown or highest score

below the ankle or with the knuckles of the index and middle fingers. The referee deducts points for penalties. Full point penalties include attacking an opponent's back, attacking an opponent's face with the hands, or throwing an opponent. Half-point penalties include pushing, grabbing, and holding. Half-point penalties count only if the referee calls a second one.

Men and women compete in separate events in four weight categories: flyweight, featherweight, welterweight, and heavyweight. If a match ends in a tie, the athlete with the most points after penalties are deducted is the winner. If a tie still exists, the referee decides the winner. If a tie exists in a gold medal match, a fourth "sudden-death" match is played. If neither athlete scores a point in this fourth round, the referee decides the winner.

In taekwondo, athletes win points by delivering strikes, such as a kick to the side of the body or the abdomen.

In the Olympics

Taekwondo first appeared as an official Olympic event at the 2000 games in Sydney, Australia. South Korean athletes won three of the eight gold medals—Jung Jae Eun (women's featherweight), Sun-Hee Lee (women's welterweight), and Kyong-Hun Kim (men's heavyweight). Other gold medalists included Michail Mouroutsos of Greece (men's flyweight), Angel Valodia Matos Fuentes of Cuba (men's welterweight), Lauren Burns of Australia (women's flyweight), and Chen Zhong of China (women's heavyweight).

With patience and a penalty point against his opponent, Steven Lopez of the United States won the men's featherweight event in 2000. Lopez faced Sin Joon Sik of South Korea for the gold medal. Lopez, who is 6 inches taller than Sin, used his height advantage to keep Sin backing away and risking penalties for his lack of aggression. With about a minute left in the final round and the match scoreless, Sin tried a kick and Lopez countered to score the winning point.

TEAM HANDBALL

Team handball is a high-speed game that combines elements of soccer and basketball. Players rely on such skills as running, jumping, catching, and throwing to score the goals that win the game. They also need speed, endurance, strength, agility, and great teamwork.

Origin of the Sport

Team handball can be traced back to ancient Greece. In his epic poem the *Odyssey*, Homer describes a game invented by a Spartan princess. Versions of the game were played by aristocrats in ancient Rome and later by knights in medieval Europe. Some historians maintain that modern team handball developed in Germany in 1897. Others claim that the game started in Sweden or Denmark in the early 1900s. Whatever its origins, team handball has been a popular sport for a long time. Although it is not widely played in the United States, the sport is played by more than 4 million people in over 120 countries.

In 1926, the International Amateur Athletic Federation appointed a committee to standardize the rules of team handball. Two years later, the International Amateur Handball

Fast Facts

First Olympic competition

Munich, Germany; 1936

Legendary athlete

Anja Andersen, **Denmark**

Criteria for winning

Scoring the most goals

As reigning champs, the Korean women's team put up a fight against Denmark at the 1996 games, but the Danes took the gold in overtime.

Federation was founded, with Avery Brundage (later IOC president) as its first president. As host of the 1936 Olympic Games, Germany opted to include team handball in competition. Dropped from the games for more than 30 years, the sport reappeared in 1972 at the games in Munich, Germany, and has been part of the Olympics ever since.

Competing in the Event

Team handball is played by two teams, each consisting of six players and a goalie. It is played indoors on a court that measures 40 meters (131 feet) long by 20 m (65 ft) wide, about 35 percent larger than a basketball court. The object of the game is to throw a hard leather ball, about 7 inches (18 centimeters) in diameter, past the goalkeeper into the opposing team's goal net. Players do this by dribbling and passing the ball down the court. They may throw the ball with their hands or propel it with any part of their body above the knee. Once a player has stopped, he or she must pass or shoot within 3 seconds.

The game is played in two 30-minute halves, with a 10-minute rest between the periods. There are no time-outs, except for injury. Although team handball is considered a noncontact sport, the fast breaks, blocks, jumps, and dives make contact unavoidable. Defensive players may check their opponents as in ice hockey, but they may not use their arms or legs to push, hold, trip, or hit other players. A player who commits a foul is suspended for two minutes.

In the Olympics

Germany, Yugoslavia, and the former Soviet Union dominated men's handball for many years. Women's team handball appeared as an Olympic sport for the first time at the 1976 games in Montreal, when both the men's and women's teams from the Soviet Union won the gold. Great women's teams have historically come from Eastern Europe and South Korea. In 1996, however, Denmark—led by Anja Andersen—beat South Korea in overtime, 37-33, in the women's final. Denmark defended its Olympic gold medal, coming back from a six-goal deficit in 2000 to beat Hungary 31-27.

TENNIS

Tennis is a sport that involves hitting a ball hard and fast over a net while preventing the opposing player from returning the ball. Players may have only a split second to return a shot coming at them at 100 miles (161 kilometers) an hour. Quick reflexes, stamina, and strategy are all important.

Origin of the Sport

The modern game of tennis began to take shape in France about 500 years ago. The French played an indoor game called *paume,* a form of handball, which consisted of swatting a cloth bag stuffed with hair back and forth with their hands. Players soon began to use rackets to help extend their reach. Nobody knows for certain how tennis came to be called "tennis." The most popular theory suggests that the name comes from the French word *tenez,* which means "take it."

In 1873, Major W.C. Wingfield, an Englishman, moved the game outdoors onto grass courts. Lawn tennis was less expensive to play than the indoor version, which had to be played in special buildings. Wingfield also simplified the rules. By the late 1870s, the sport had become enormously popular and tennis clubs opened throughout the world. The first organized tennis tournament was held at the All-England Croquet and Lawn Tennis Club, the site of today's Wimbledon.

Tennis came to the United States in 1874, when Mary Outerbridge learned the game while vacationing in Bermuda. Outerbridge promoted the game through her efforts to establish a lawn tennis court on the grounds of the Staten Island Cricket and Baseball Club. The game caught on quickly, and Outerbridge's success led to the establishment of the U.S. Lawn Tennis Association. In 1900, Dwight F. Davis, a recent graduate of Harvard University, started the International Lawn Tennis Challenge Trophy, now known as the Davis Cup.

In 1967, Texas oilman Lamar Hunt changed tennis by offering prize money to persuade many top players to leave the amateur circuit. In 1968, when Wimbledon officials realized that their prestigious event was going to be held without the world's top players, they agreed to pay players, too. As soon as Wimbledon offered prize money, all other tournaments did

Fast Facts

First Olympic competition

Athens, Greece; 1896

Legendary athletes

Suzanne Lenglen, **France**
Venus Williams, **USA**

Criteria for winning

Best of two or three sets

as well. That began a new era in tennis, whose major events are now open to both amateur and professional players.

Competing in the Event

Men and women compete in singles or doubles matches. In singles, one player competes against another. In doubles, two players compete against two other players. The object of the game is to hit the ball in a way that prevents the opposing player(s) from returning it. The server puts the ball into play by hitting it into the service box on the opposite side of the net. A player wins a point if his or her opponent fails to return the ball before it touches the ground twice on the opponent's side of the net. A player also wins a point when the opposing player returns the ball so that it hits outside the boundaries of the court.

Tennis is scored in games and sets. To win a game, a player must score four points and win by at least two. The first player to win six games, by a margin of two, wins the set. If a set is tied after six games, a tiebreaker is played. Men's and women's matches are won by the first player or pair to win the best of five sets (men) or the best of three sets (women).

A tennis court measures 78 feet (23.77 meters) long and is divided in half by the net, which is 3 ft (0.91 m) high at the center. Singles courts are 27 ft (8.22 m) wide, and doubles courts are 36 ft (11 m) wide. Before the 1960s, all tennis rackets were made of wood. In the late 1960s, aluminum rackets began replacing the wooden ones, and this gave players more power. By the late 1970s, most of the world's top players were using metal rackets. Soon companies began making rackets out of graphite, a lighter and stiffer metal, and players were able to hit with still more power. Today, serves charge over the net at speeds greater than 100 miles (161 km) per hour.

In the Olympics

Tennis was an Olympic sport from 1896 to 1924. Irish-born John Boland won the first gold medal for Great Britain, in singles, and then won the men's doubles with a German partner, Fritz Traun. Boland protested when the English flag was raised for his victory, so an Irish flag was raised instead.

FUZZY WUZZY

Have you ever wondered why tennis balls are fuzzy? Tennis balls are covered with felt material for two reasons. First, the fuzzy texture of the material slows down the ball and makes it possible to return a shot. Second, fuzz enables the racket strings to grip the ball, helping players to hit it with top-spin or backspin.

In 1900, the women's singles event was added, and Charlotte Cooper of Great Britain became the first woman to win a medal in any Olympic sport. The 1920 games featured Suzanne Lenglen of France—one of the greatest women tennis players ever—who lost only four games in the ten sets it took to win the singles gold medal. That year, the women's doubles event was added, and Great Britain won the gold and silver medals. The United States dominated the 1924 tennis events, winning five of the six gold medals.

Tennis was then dropped from the Olympic program because of the difficulty distinguishing between amateur and professional players. It returned to the Olympics in 1988, when Steffi Graf of West Germany and Miloslav Mecir of Czechoslovakia won the first Olympic tennis singles gold medals in 64 years. Just a week before the Olympics, Graf had won the U.S. Open to sweep the Grand Slam (winning the four major world tennis tournaments—the French Open, the Australian Open, Wimbledon, and the U.S. Open). At the 1992 games, Graf lost to American Jennifer Capriati.

American Zina Garrison sets up a serve during a match at the 1988 games in Seoul. Garrison won the bronze medal.

Although Lindsay Davenport had never advanced past the quarterfinals in any major tennis tournament to that time, she lost only one set in six matches to capture the singles gold at the 1996 games in Atlanta, Georgia. Davenport faced her best friend, Mary Joe Fernandez, in the semifinals. Following her stunning victory, Davenport apologized to her friend as they shook hands at the net.

Professional tennis players have been allowed to participate in Olympic Games since 1992. Singles gold medal winners have included Marc Rossett of Switzerland; Yevgeni Kafelnikov of Russia; and Andre Agassi, Jennifer Capriati, and Lindsay Davenport of the United States.

At the 2000 Summer Olympics in Sydney, Australia, Venus Williams, who had won Wimbledon and the U.S. Open that year, captured the singles gold medal, defeating Elena Dementieva of Russia, 6-2, 6-4. Then, joined by her sister Serena, she took the doubles gold for the United States.

TRACK AND FIELD

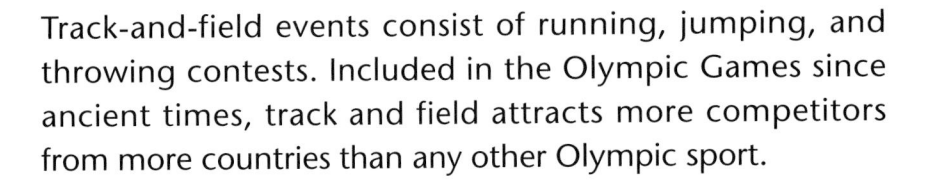

Track-and-field events consist of running, jumping, and throwing contests. Included in the Olympic Games since ancient times, track and field attracts more competitors from more countries than any other Olympic sport.

Origin of the Sport

Soon after humans began running, jumping, and throwing things for survival, they probably began to compete with one another to see who could run faster, jump higher, and throw farther. The first Olympiad consisted of a single track event—a race of about 200 yards (183 meters). By the 13th Olympiad, more events had been added, including discus throwing, boxing, wrestling, and chariot racing. Field events also have a long history, existing in many cultures. Around the time of Jesus, Celtic warriors in Ireland had to take a high-jump test to prove their fitness to protect the king. The Vikings were known to have practiced hammer throwing as early as A.D. 800. In the late 1700s, Germans developed a stand with holes and pegs to support a bar for high jumping.

The first running track in England was built in 1837. It consisted of a narrow gravel path that allowed for only two-man races. Track racing went indoors in 1861, when the first indoor meet was held in Cincinnati, Ohio. Technology has greatly affected modern track events. Electronic and photo-finish timekeeping have become the standard for today's contests.

Competing in the Event

Track-and-field events, sometimes called athletics, are held on a 400-m (437-yd) oval track and in a separate area nearby. Many different activities comprise the sport. Track events are running races, either flat or with hurdles, categorized by length—sprints (100 to 400 m), middle-distance (800 to 1,500 m), and long-distance (5,000 m to the marathon, which is a grueling 26 miles long).

Speed and a good start are key in sprint races. Racing competitors run in separate lanes. Because runners in the outside lanes have a longer distance to run around the

Fast Facts

First Olympic competition

Athens, Greece; 1896

Legendary athletes

Sebastian Coe, **Great Britain**

Mildred "Babe" Didrikson, **USA**

Jackie Joyner-Kersee, **USA**

Kip Keino, **Kenya**

Paavo Nurmi, **Finland**

Jesse Owens, **USA**

Jim Thorpe, **USA**

Emil Zátopek, **Czechoslovakia**

Criteria for winning

Fastest time, longest or highest distance, most points scored curves, they line up in starting blocks a little farther down the track. In a kneeling position, runners set their feet against metal blocks. At the "set" command, runners raise their knees, and when the gun sounds, they push off hard. The athletes then lengthen their strides and run at full speed to the finish line. Sprint races last from less than 10 seconds for the 100-m dash to 49 seconds for the 400-m.

Middle-distance runners circle the track twice for the 800-m and nearly four times for the 1,500-m. Middle-distance races generally last from less than two minutes to about four minutes. In these contests, competitors must be fast enough to gain an advantage, but they must also be able to conserve energy for the final push to the finish line. Even an athlete in great physical shape can run at full speed for only about 100 m before his or her muscles use all the available oxygen.

Middle-distance racers start in lanes. In the 800-m race, runners stay in their lanes through the first turn, and then they cut to the inside of the track as quickly as they can to shorten the total distance they must run. The 1,500-m race is probably the most popular of the middle-distance runs. It is known as the metric mile because it is just 120 yards shy of a mile.

Distance runners strive for a smooth and efficient pace. To conserve energy, they barely move their arms, take shorter strides than sprinters, and land softly on their feet. Competitors stay close together in a pack and then try to break away with a burst of speed when the race is almost over. The long-distance races last from just over 13 minutes for the 5,000-m race to nearly 2.5 hours for the marathon.

At just over 26 miles (42 km), the marathon is the longest Olympic running race. The marathon is run on a road course, often through city streets. At the Olympics, the marathon begins and ends with a lap around the stadium track. Marathon runners need plenty of water during the race, so water stations are placed at intervals throughout the course. Some marathon runners burst ahead during the early miles, hoping to hold their lead through the remaining distance. Others save their energy for the final miles so they can increase their speed and try to pass the leaders.

In relay races, teams of four pass a baton from one runner to the next. In the 4×100-m relay event, each runner sprints 100 m before passing the baton to the next teammate. In

The indisputable star of the 1984 games in Los Angeles, Carl Lewis won Olympic gold in three races and in the long jump.

the 4×400-m relay, each person runs 400 m. The baton is passed in an area called the passing zone, which is 20 m long. A team that passes its baton outside the zone is disqualified.

Hurdles require great skill and a combination of speed and balance. In the 100-m (for women) and 110-m (for men), hurdlers sprint straight down the track while jumping over ten obstacles. Hurdles are 33 inches (0.76 m) high for women and 42 inches (1.67 m) high for men. The 400-m hurdles event is known as the "man killer" because it is so physically demanding.

The 3,000-m steeplechase (for men only) is a special hurdling event. The course is slightly less than two miles long, and athletes must make it over 28 hurdles and 7 water jumps. A 3-ft (0.91 m) hurdle stands in front of a pool of water at each water jump. The hurdles are heavy and solidly built to prevent them from being knocked over. The pool is 12 ft (3.7 m) square and about 27 inches (70 centimeters) deep. Runners step on or jump over the hurdle, land in the water, and then leap onto dry land. With few exceptions, most notably KIP KEINO of Kenya, steeplechase competitors are specialists in the event. They generally do not compete in other events.

Field events consist of the high jump, long jump, triple jump, pole vault, shot put, discus throw, hammer throw, and javelin. In addition, all-around athletes compete in the heptathlon (for women) and the decathlon (for men). These multi-event contests combine seven and ten events, respectively, and emphasize endurance and versatility.

In the high jump, the athlete propels his or her body over a bar. Contestants can choose any style to clear the bar, but they must jump off from one foot. They run toward the bar along a semicircular path, gaining the momentum that will lift them up and over. High jumpers currently clear a bar that is more than 7 ft (2.1 m) above the ground. An athlete jumps until he or she misses three attempts at a particular height. The best height cleared is the one that counts.

The long jumper starts by sprinting down a runway to a board at the end. On the last step, the jumper tries to hit the board with one foot and launch into the air. Long jumpers cover a distance of about 28 ft (8.5 m). The athlete lands in a

PROFILES IN COURAGE

Not every winner at the Olympics earns a gold medal. Many athletes win simply by doing their best. In 1968, Tanzania's John Stephen Akhwari, his right leg bloody and bandaged after an injury, staggered into the stadium more than an hour behind the winner of the marathon. "My country did not send me to Mexico City to start the race," he said. "They sent me to finish the race."

At the 1968 games in Mexico City, Bob Beamon of the United States flew through the air in what became the most famous long jump—29 feet, 2½ inches. Beamon's world record remained unbroken until 1991.

pit filled with sand. The length of the jump is measured from the edge of the takeoff board to the closest mark made in the sand. Each jumper has six attempts, but only the longest jump counts.

Triple jumpers use the same runway as long jumpers, but they start from much farther back. They also must launch themselves from a takeoff board. The triple jump, known as the hop, step, and jump, begins with a running start. The athlete then leaps off one foot and lands on the same foot (the hop). The jumper's momentum continues with a giant stride onto the opposite foot (the step). Then, using the same foot, he pushes off the takeoff board and launches into the air (the jump). Champion triple jumpers can cover close to 60 ft (18 m). The length of the jump is measured from the takeoff board to the closest mark made in the sandpit where the jumper finally lands. Triple jumpers also get six attempts; the best jump counts in the final standings.

Pole vaulters use a fiberglass pole to clear a bar that is balanced between two supports. After sprinting down a runway with the long pole, the athlete jams the far end of the pole into a box. The vaulter's speed and body weight make the pole bend. As the pole begins to straighten, the athlete swings and lifts his or her body until it is above the pole. Athletes soar more than 19 ft (5.8 m) in the air. The pole continues to straighten as it flings the vaulter over the bar. A vaulter is given three attempts to clear a height.

The discus is a flat, saucer-shaped disc made of wood and metal. The men's discus is about 9 inches (22 cm) in diameter and weighs about 4.5 pounds (2 kilograms). The women's discus is about 7 inches (18 cm) in diameter and weighs about 2 lb (1 kg). Athletes throw the discus from an 8-ft circle. If the thrower steps outside the circle, the throw is not counted. Athletes hold the discus flat against their palm and forearm, with their fingertips curled around the edge. The thrower spins one and a half times while swinging the discus with a straight arm. Then, using strength and momentum from the spin, the athlete hurls the discus—often more than 200 feet!

In the shot put, competitors "put," or push, a metal ball from shoulder level. The athlete holds the shot (ball) with one hand resting against his or her shoulder. Facing away from the throwing area, the athlete turns, bends forward, and then hops backward across the circle on one leg. On the second hop, the athlete turns and puts the shot. The men's shot weighs 16 lb (7 kg), and the women's shot weighs around 9 lb (4 kg). Athletes may not step outside the throwing circle.

The javelin, a long shaft with a sharp metal point at one end, is thrown for distance. Carrying this spearlike instrument, the athlete sprints down a runway. Just before reaching the foul line, the thrower plants his or her front foot and throws the javelin from above shoulder level. The tip of the javelin must break the surface of the ground when it lands. The throw is measured from the edge of the foul line to the point where the javelin breaks the ground. Throwers have six attempts, and only the longest throw counts.

A 16-lb (7.3-kg) metal ball attached to a handle by a steel wire is used for the hammer throw. The thrower uses both hands to swing the hammer in circles, so that it passes below his knees and above his head. After several turns, which generate more force, the athlete lets go, sending the hammer flying about 260 ft (79 m). Before the 2000 games, only men competed in the hammer throw.

The heptathlon and the decathlon are two-day events that combine the most difficult sprint races, jumps, throws, and endurance runs into a single competition. The heptathlon, for women only, consists of the 100-m hurdles, high jump, shot put, and 200-m dash. The second day's events are the long jump, javelin throw, and 800-m run.

The decathlon, which is for men only, consists of the 100-m dash, long jump, shot put, high jump, and 400-m dash on the first day. On the second day, athletes compete in the 110-m hurdles, discus throw, pole vault, javelin throw, and 1,500-m run.

In both competitions, athletes earn points based on their performance in each event. The athletes compete against one another, but they also try to perform as well as they can to earn the greatest number of points. The competitor who scores the most points in all the events combined wins.

SHOWING THEIR STRENGTH

Sixteen years after the IOC declared that women were strong enough to compete in a marathon, the committee opened six more events to female athletes. At the 2000 games in Sydney, women were allowed to compete for the first time in modern pentathlon, hammer throw, pole vault, water polo, weightlifting, and track cycling.

SAFETY FIRST

In 1986, javelins were modified to reduce the distance they could be thrown. Before the modification, javelins were being thrown such a great distance that Olympic officials feared for the safety of spectators and runners on the track.

In the Olympics

Track and field is the oldest Olympic sport, dating back to the ancient games. Since the modern Olympics were first held in 1896, English-speaking countries have dominated the sprint events. The men's 100-m dash has been contested 25 times, and 23 times the winner came from an English-speaking country, including 16 from the United States alone. American sprinters have won the 200-m title 16 times and the 400-m 18 times. Among the great American male sprinters who have won both the 100-m and 200-m races are Archie Hahn (1904), Ralph Craig (1912), Eddie Tolan (1932), JESSE OWENS (1936), Bobby Morrow (1956), and Carl Lewis (1984). At the 1968 games in Mexico City, U.S. sprinter Lee Evan won the 400-m in 43.86 seconds—a record that would last for 19 years.

At the 1996 games in Atlanta, Michael Johnson, the current world record holder in the 200-m and 400-m, became the first man to win gold medals in both events at the Olympics. At the 2000 games in Sydney, Johnson won another gold medal in the 400-m, becoming the first man ever to win that event in consecutive Olympiads. Johnson won his fifth career gold medal running the anchor leg for the American 4×400-m relay team. That same year, Konstantinos Kenteris won the 200-m sprint to become the first Greek man to win a gold medal in running since Spyridon Louis won the marathon in 1896 in Athens.

The U.S. men have dominated the hurdles, too, winning 19 of a possible 25 gold medals in the 110-m and 17 out of 22 in the 400-m. Great American hurdlers who successfully defended their gold medals were Lee Calhoun (1956 and 1960) and Roger Kingdom (1984 and 1988) in the 110-m, and Glenn Davis (1956 and 1960) in the 400-m. Edwin Moses captured the gold medal in the 400-m hurdles in 1976 and 1984, but the U.S. boycott of the 1980 games in Moscow cost Moses his chance for a third gold medal.

American women have triumphed as well. Wilma Rudolph (1960), Florence Griffith Joyner (1988), and Marion Jones (2000) each won gold medals in both the 100-m and 200-m sprints. With three gold and two bronze medals, Jones became the first female athlete to win five medals in track and field in a single Olympiad.

U.S. sprinter Valerie Brisco-Hooks pulled off a rare double by finishing in first place in the 200-m and 400-m sprints in 1984 in Los Angeles. Wyomia Tyus and Gail Devers are the only female sprinters in Olympic history to win consecutive gold medals in the 100-m dash. Tyus did it in 1964 and 1968, Devers in 1992 and 1996.

The bright star of the 1948 games in London was FANNY BLANKERS-KOEN, who won gold medals in the 100-m dash, 200-m dash, 80-m hurdles, and the 4×100 team relay. The daughter of a Dutch farmer, Koen began her Olympic career when she was 18. By 1948, she held six world records.

PAAVO NURMI of Finland dominated middle-distance running in the 1920s. He won nine gold medals and three silver medals at the games in 1920, 1924, and 1928. At the 1952 games in Helsinki, Finland, EMIL ZÁTOPEK of Czechoslovakia won the 5,000- and 10,000-m runs, as well as the marathon. No one before or since has won those three races at one Olympics.

New Zealand's Peter Snell won a surprise victory in the 800-m in 1960, and then captured the gold medal in both the 800-m and the 1,500-m races in 1964. No runner since Snell has successfully defended an Olympic 800-m title. At the 1984 games in Los Angeles and the 1988 games in Seoul, Sebastian Coe of Great Britain won gold medals in the 1,500-m and silver medals in the 800-m. At the 1976 games in Montreal, Alberto Juantorena of Cuba captured a rare double by winning the gold medal in both the 400- and the 800-m races.

Florence Griffith-Joyner's stunning performance at the 1988 games in Seoul won her three gold medals and one silver.

Lasse Viren of Finland achieved perhaps the most remarkable double-double in Olympic history by winning the 5,000-m and 10,000-m runs in both 1972 and 1976. In recent years, Ethiopian runners have triumphed in these two events. Miruts Yifter won the 5,000-m and 10,000-m runs in 1980, and Haile Gebrselassie won the gold in the 10,000-m in 1996 and 2000. At the Sydney games, Gebrselassie crossed the finish line like a sprinter to defeat Paul Tergat of Kenya by 0.009 of a second. It was the closest race in Olympic history in this event. Kenyan runners have also won their share of races. Kenyans won the 3,000-m steeplechase in five consecutive Olympiads, beginning in 1984.

THE FIRST MARATHON

The marathon draws its inspiration from a legendary runner named Phidippides, who was sent to Athens in 490 B.C. to deliver the news of the Greek victory at the battle of Marathon. According to the story, Phidippides arrived and delivered his news. He then collapsed and died from exhaustion.

The middle-distance and long-distance races are relatively new Olympic events for women. At the 1928 games in Amsterdam, several women collapsed after the 800-m race. Officials decided that women were too weak to race more than 200 m and dropped women's distance races from the program. Then in 1962, the 800-m race was reinstated. In 1964, the 400-m was introduced; and in 1972, a 1,500-m event was added to the games. The women's 5,000-m race is a relatively new event for women. It replaces the 3,000-m race, which was run from 1984 to 1992. Now women run the same races as the men, with the exception of the steeplechase.

Only two runners have won the marathon in consecutive Olympiads—ABEBE BIKILA of Ethiopia (1960 and 1964) and Waldemar Cierpinski of East Germany (1976 and 1980). Frank Shorter of the United States won the marathon gold in 1972 and the silver in 1976. Ethiopia has won four men's marathons in the Olympics—more than any other nation.

Women were not permitted to run the marathon in the Olympics until 1984. That year, Joan Benoit of the United States won the first-ever women's Olympic marathon. Norway's Grete Waitz won the silver medal. The women's 10,000-m race was added in 1988, when Rosa Mota of Portugal won the gold.

RAY EWRY dominated the Olympic men's jumping events during the early 1900s. Ewry won a total of ten individual gold medals in the standing long jump, standing triple jump, and standing high jump. No other Olympic athlete had ever won that many medals.

The United States has always dominated the long jump, winning the gold medal 21 out of a possible 25 times. William DeHart Hubbard became the first African-American athlete to win an Olympic gold medal in an individual event when he won the long jump in Paris in 1924. Bob Beamon won the gold medal in the long jump at the 1968 games in Mexico City. He broke the world record by almost 2 ft with an amazing leap of more than 29 ft. In doing so, he set a record that would stand for 23 years. Carl Lewis won the long jump in four consecutive Olympiads—1984, 1988, 1992, and 1996.

In 1968, gold medalist Dick Fosbury of the United States revolutionized high jumping when he introduced the "Fosbury flop." Before the maneuver, most jumpers rolled sideways over the bar facedown. This was called the Western Roll. With the flop, Fosbury threw himself over the bar headfirst with his face up. With this innovative technique, athletes jump with their back to the bar. Cuba's Javier Sotomayor, who in 1989 became the first person to high jump 8 ft using this method, won the gold medal in 1992. Sotomayor, who still holds the world record of 8 ft, ½ inch (2.45 m) set in 1993, earned a silver medal in Sydney in 2000.

Between 1896 and 1968, athletes from the United States won every official Olympic pole vault competition. These 16 consecutive gold medals represent the longest national winning streak in any event in any sport in Olympic history. The streak was finally broken at the Munich games in 1972. The defending champion, American Bob Seagren, came in second after officials banned the use of the pole preferred by Seagren and several other leading vaulters. The dispute was over the materials used in manufacturing the pole, as well as the fact that the poles were not readily available to all competitors.

Throwing events for men have been part of every Olympiad since 1896. The first throwing event for women—the discus—was added in 1928. Four years later, the javelin was added. The women's shot put became part of the Olympic program in 1948.

Dick Fosbury revolutionized high jump technique at the 1968 games in Mexico City by throwing himself over the bar head first. This method of "flopping" over the bar became known as the "Fosbury flop."

BREAKING RECORDS MORE EASILY

BREAKING RECORDS MORE EASILY

Companies that manufacture sports equipment spend millions of dollars designing lighter running shoes, slippery bathing suits that enable swimmers to glide through the water more quickly, and better track surfaces for runners. Fans may not realize, for example, that today's pole vaulters use springy fiberglass poles instead of the less flexible steel poles that were used years ago.

Martin Sheridan of the United States won the discus gold medal in 1904, 1906, and 1908. In all, Sheridan earned five gold medals and four silver medals in discus and shot put. AL OERTER of the United States is the only athlete ever to win the same Olympic track-and-field event four consecutive times. He earned four gold medals in the discus throw.

BABE DIDRIKSON qualified for all five individual women's track-and-field events at the 1932 games in Los Angeles, but IOC restrictions allowed her to compete in only three of them. She won gold medals in the javelin throw and the 80-m hurdles, and a silver medal in the high jump.

Multi-event competitions were held in some of the Olympic Games in ancient Greece. In 708 B.C., the first known pentathlon was held. The pentathlon combined five events—javelin, discus, long jump, wrestling, and a footrace.

The decathlon made its debut in the modern Olympic Games in 1904. That year, the event was called "The All-Around Championship," and the ten events were held on the same day. The legendary JIM THORPE of the United States won gold medals in both the pentathlon and the decathlon at the 1912 games in Stockholm, Sweden.

In 1948, at the age of 17, Bob Mathias of the United States became the youngest decathlon winner in Olympic history. Four years later he repeated his victory, setting a world record and becoming the first man to win back-to-back gold medals in the decathlon. In 1960, American Rafer Johnson defeated his former college teammate, C.K. Yang of Taiwan, in the decathlon. Johnson returned to the Olympic stadium in 1984 when he served as the final torchbearer at the Opening Ceremony of the Los Angeles games. Bruce Jenner won the decathlon at the 1976 games in Montreal, Canada, by one of the largest margins in Olympic history. With victories in 1980 and 1984, Daley Thompson of Great Britain became the second man in Olympic history to win back-to-back gold medals in the decathlon.

Women competed in a five-event pentathlon from 1960 to 1980. In 1984, two events were added to make the contest a heptathlon. American athlete JACKIE JOYNER-KERSEE is the most successful female multisport competitor. She won a silver medal in the heptathlon in 1984 and then won back-to-back gold medals in the event in 1988 and 1992.

TRIATHLON

The triathlon is a three-sport endurance race that combines swimming, cycling, and running. Competitors complete the three events in sequence with only brief slowdowns, called transitions, to change clothing and equipment.

Origin of the Sport

Although the triathlon as we know it today is a relative newcomer to the sports scene, the 1904 Olympiad featured a three-event competition called a triathlon. It consisted of a long jump, shot put, and 100-yard dash. The modern triathlon was developed in 1974 by a group of distance runners in San Diego, California. Looking for a way to make their training routines more fun and more interesting, they established the first known swim-cycle-run race.

In 1977, John Collins, a triathlete and U.S. naval officer, was stationed in the Hawaiian Islands. He and several of his fellow officers wanted to find out who among them was a real "iron man." In doing so, they created the now-famous Ironman competition, which has been held in Oahu, one of the Hawaiian Islands, since 1978. The Ironman combines three annual endurance events: the Waikiki Roughwater Swim (2.4 miles/3.8 km), the Around Oahu Bike Ride (112 miles/180 km), and the Honolulu Marathon (26.2 miles/42 km). Only 12 of the 15 participants completed the first Ironman competition. The following year, 15 athletes (including one woman) competed.

In 1989, the International Triathlon Union (ITU) was founded in France, and the first official triathlon world championship occurred there. In 1993, the Pan American Games approved the event for inclusion in the 1995 competitions in Argentina. Then in 1994, the IOC voted to include the triathlon as a medal sport at the 2000 games in Sydney.

Competing in the Event

Although known as a short-course triathlon, the Olympic event is anything but short. Triathletes begin with a 1.5-km (0.93-mile) swim in open water, followed by a 40-km (24.9-mile) bicycle ride, and ending with a 10-km (6.2-mile) run.

Fast Facts

First Olympic competition

Sydney, Australia; 2000

Legendary athletes

Brigitte McMahon, **Switzerland**

Simon Whitfield, **Canada**

Criteria for winning

Fastest time

Racers must wear swim caps during the open-water swim. If the water temperature is below 14°C (57.2°F), they must also wear wetsuits. Between 14°C and 20°C, wetsuits are optional, and above 20°C (68°F), they are prohibited. During the cycling portion of the triathlon, racers wear helmets and shirts to cover their torsos. Cyclists, who ride lightweight, 16-speed bicycles, cannot draft—ride directly behind another cyclist who blocks the wind—for more than 15 seconds.

In the Olympics

The 50 athletes who participated in the triathlon in 2000 qualified through their world rankings. Each country is limited to three competitors per event.

Australians especially love and excel in the triathlon, which may explain why the event was given such a prominent place on the Olympic schedule. The women's triathlon was the opening event of the Sydney games. Brigitte McMahon of Switzerland captured the gold medal, pulling ahead of Australian favorite Michellie Jones in the last 100 m. McMahon's time was 2 hours, 40 seconds. Jones finished a mere 2 seconds later.

The following day, Simon Whitfield of Canada won the men's event in a dramatic recovery after colliding with 15 others in the cycling portion. With 800 m to go in the 10-km run, Whitfield was behind Germany's Stephan Vuckovic, who was then in first place. Whitfield caught up to Vuckovic in the last 200 m and finished the race in 1 hour 48 minutes and 24 seconds. Vuckovic finished 13.56 seconds behind him.

The triathlon is fast and intense for competitors and exciting for spectators. The meteoric rise in interest in the sport suggests that it will be a significant part of the Olympic Games for many years to come.

In the first Olympic triathlon, Switzerland's Brigitte McMahon raises her arms in celebration as she crosses the finish line in the women's competition.

VOLLEYBALL

Both an indoor and outdoor game, volleyball involves two teams hitting a ball over a net with their arms and hands. The game's most aggressive move, which is often impossible to return, is the spike.

Origin of the Sport

William Morgan, a YMCA instructor in Holyoke, Massachusetts, invented volleyball in 1895. He created the game primarily for middle-aged businessmen as a lively alternative to calisthenics (repetitive gymnastic exercises). Morgan initially used a badminton net and called the new sport mintonette. In 1896, Dr. Alfred Halstead (a colleague of Morgan's) renamed the game volleyball because this name better described the essential nature of the sport—volleying a ball back and forth over the net. Volleyball spread quickly for several reasons. It was a simple game with easily achievable goals. In addition, the YM-YWCA enthusiastically promoted the game in its chapters throughout the world.

The Volleyball Rules Committee of the YMCA presided over the first national championship in Brooklyn, New York, in 1922. Then, in 1928, the United States Volleyball Association (now USA Volleyball) was formed to create the official guidelines for the sport and to schedule national tournaments. American soldiers played volleyball in Europe during World War I, and the game took off in France and Russia. The first international tournament took place in Paris in 1931. The international governing body of the sport, the Federation Internationale de Volley-Ball (FIVB), was founded in Paris in 1947. Ten years later the IOC designated volleyball as an Olympic sport to be included at the 1964 games in Tokyo, Japan.

Competing in the Event

Two teams of six players each play volleyball on a court that measures 59 feet (18 meters) long and 29.5 ft (9 m) wide. A net divides the court into two halves. The net is nearly 8 ft (2.4 m) high for men and slightly over 7 ft (2.2 m) for women. The

Fast Facts

First Olympic competition

Tokyo, Japan; 1964

Legendary athlete

Karch Kiraly, USA

Criteria for winning

Best three of five games

BEACH VOLLEYBALL

Played according to the same basic rules as the indoor game, beach volleyball is played on sand. Athletes compete barefoot and cannot jump as high as they can on an indoor court. Conditioning is especially important because it is more difficult to move quickly in sand. Beach volleyball is one of the fastest-growing sports in the world. Two-person men's and women's beach volleyball became Olympic events in 1996.

standard volleyball, slightly smaller than a basketball, weighs about 9 to 10 ounces (260 to 280 grams) and is between 25 and 27 inches (62 and 67 centimeters) in circumference.

Play begins after a coin toss to determine which team serves first. Teams position three players in the front row near the net and three players on the back line. Each player on the serving team rotates clockwise one position after the serve. The opposing team must return the ball over the net in three or fewer hits without letting it touch the ground. If the ball touches the ground within the boundaries of the court, the opposing team is awarded one point. Players may use any part of their body to send the ball back over the net. They can use one or both hands to hit the ball, as well as a clenched fist. Players may not throw, catch, lift, push, or scoop the ball, and no player may hit the ball twice in a row. If the ball touches the top of the net and then goes over, it is still in play.

In competitive volleyball, most service returns are passes to teammates. One player fields the serve by hitting the ball into the air with an underhand bump. The second player sets the ball by hitting it into the air. A third player spikes the ball over the net. Spiking requires excellent timing and jumping. To spike, a hitter jumps high in the air, reaches to the ball above the net, and powerfully drives it downward into the opponent's court.

Meanwhile, on the other side of the net, defensive players rush into positions to anticipate the spike. The first line of defense consists of the blockers. Two or three players jump and try to block the spike with their arms. A block does not count as one of a team's three hits. If a spike eludes the blockers, other defensive players dive and roll on the ground to dig the ball before it bounces off the floor. The first team to score 25 points (with a 2-point margin) wins the game. A team must win three games to win a match. If a match goes to a deciding fifth set, the final set is played to 15 points.

In the Olympics

Volleyball first appeared as an Olympic event, for both men and women, at the 1964 Summer Olympics in Tokyo, Japan. The Japanese proved to be a powerful and innovative force. The women's team captured the gold, and the men took the

The U.S. men's volleyball team won the gold at the 1984 Los Angeles games, due in part to the skills of team captain Karch Kiraly.

bronze. Of special interest to spectators and other players was the Japanese version of the "rolling retrieve." This is a spectacular move in which a player dives in order to hit an incoming ball that may be several feet away. The player then rolls over and jumps back up to join the ongoing play. The rolling retrieve is executed with such speed and grace that it seems like one lightning-fast, flowing move. In 1968, the Japanese men's team won the silver medal, and in 1972 they captured the gold. Japanese women won the silver in 1968 and 1972, the gold in 1976, and the bronze in 1984.

Even though volleyball originated in the United States, neither the men's nor the women's team won an Olympic medal until 1984. That year, the men's squad, led by the legendary Karch Kiraly, won the gold medal, and the women took the silver. American men, with Kiraly, went on to win the gold again in 1988, joining the former Soviet Union as one of the only two countries to have won the men's competition in successive Olympiads. Kiraly received special recognition for his skills and contributions to the sport when the FIVB named him Best Volleyball Player in the World in 1986 and 1988. The U.S. squad entered the 1992 Olympics hoping to pull off a "three-peat," despite the loss of Kiraly (who had moved on to compete in beach volleyball championships). Instead, the athletes had to settle for the bronze medal.

Winners of four gold medals, Soviet women have dominated the field. Between 1964 and 1984, the Russian women lost only 2 of 28 matches. The Cuban women's team, led by Mireya Luis and Magalys Carvajal, won three consecutive gold medals—1992, 1996, and 2000.

WATER POLO

Water polo is like soccer played in a swimming pool. The aim is to throw the ball past the opponent's goalie and into the net. A goal, which counts as one point, may be scored using any part of the body except a clenched fist.

Origin of the Sport

Water polo originated during a slump in competitive swimming in the late 1800s. Events had become monotonous and attendance was at an all time low. Promoters looked for a new game that would revive interest in water sports. Early water polo players straddled wooden barrels floating in the water and whacked the ball with paddles. Soon, however, players stopped using the paddles and barrels.

Initially played in lakes and ponds, water polo moved indoors in the 1880s. The game was so brutal and physically demanding that colleges banned it from competition in the early 1900s. Two important developments in the 1920s made water polo safer and helped it gain acceptance. The first was the use of larger and deeper pools, forcing players to improve their swimming skills. The second was the method of passing

Fast Facts

First Olympic competition

Paris, France; 1900

Legendary athletes

Manuel Estiarte, **Spain**

Dezsö Gyarmati, **Hungary**

Criteria for winning

Most goals scored

To distinguish the players in the pool, one team wears blue caps, the other team wears white, and the goalies wear red.

the ball from player to player without letting it touch the water, which was developed in Hungary.

Competing in the Event

Each team has seven players—six fielders and a goalie. Games consist of four 7-minute periods during which players swim as they battle for control of the ball. Field players may use only one hand to pass and shoot the ball, and they are not allowed to touch the walls or the bottom of the pool. The goalie is the only player who may touch the ball with both hands and stand on the pool bottom. Players dribble by swimming with the ball in front of them. With several hard "eggbeater" kicks, a player can rise out of the water to his waist to fire a shot at more than 50 miles (80.5 kilometers) per hour.

The pool measures 30 meters (98 feet) by 26 m (84 ft) and the water must be at least 1.8 m (about 6 ft) deep. During play, a team has 35 seconds to score. If it does not shoot in that time, the other team takes possession of the ball. After one team has scored a goal, the other team resumes play from the center of the pool. The game is rough and physical contact is common. Referees call three types of fouls. Ordinary fouls, which include holding the ball underwater, hitting the ball with a clenched fist, or pushing an opponent, result in a free throw for the other team. Exclusion fouls include kicking or striking an opponent, holding him underwater, and committing an act of excessive roughness. A player who commits an exclusion foul is removed from the game for 20 seconds, until a goal is scored, or until his own team regains possession of the ball. A penalty foul is called when a player commits a foul within 4 m of the goal and the referee decides that the foul prevented a probable goal. The other team takes a shot from the 4-m line.

In the Olympics

Hungary has won the most Olympic medals—7 gold out of a total of 13 medals. Dezsö Gyarmati ranks among the greatest of the Hungarian players, winning medals in five Olympiads. Manuel Estiarte, star of Spain's water polo team in 1992 and 1996, ended his career after 6 Olympics and 127 goals.

POLITICS IN THE POOL

More than medals were at stake at the 1956 games when the Hungarian team competed against the team from the Soviet Union. Several weeks earlier, Soviet troops had invaded Hungary, brutally suppressing an uprising against communist rule. The bitter feelings carried over into the pool, and hostilities erupted during the match. The game turned into an underwater melee and was stopped by the referee. Hungary was credited with the victory, and police were called in to prevent further rioting.

WEIGHTLIFTING

First Olympic competition

Athens, Greece; 1896

Legendary athletes

Vasily Alexeyev,
Soviet Union

Naim Suleymanoglu,
Turkey

Criteria for winning

Most weight lifted

Although weightlifting is one of the world's oldest sports, the modern sport tests only two moves—the snatch and the clean and jerk. Weightlifters use strength, speed, flexibility, balance, and coordination to lift a metal bar loaded with weights.

Origin of the Sport

Ancient wall paintings suggest that weightlifting was practiced thousands of years ago for entertainment, preparation for battle, and competition. In the 1700s in Europe, professional strongmen became a popular attraction in traveling sideshows and music halls. Weightlifting did not really become a competitive sport until the 1860s, when clubs for exceptionally strong men first appeared. These athletes used barbells that consisted of a metal bar with balls at each end made of solid iron or filled with sand. Because the weights could not be adjusted, rankings were determined by lifting certain weights a number of times. M.M. Pelletier Monnier of France developed the first set of disc-loading weights, and the Milo Barbell Company began producing barbells with interchangeable plates in 1905.

After its inclusion at the 1896 Olympic Games in Athens, weightlifting lost its image as a circus event and gained respectability. The first official world championships were held in Vienna in 1898. The formation of the International Weightlifting Federation in 1920 gave the sport official status.

Competing in the Event

Olympic weightlifters, traditionally men, compete in weight classes ranging from bantamweight at 119 pounds (54 kilograms) to superheavyweight at more than 238 lb (108 kg). The women's Olympic weightlifting competition was introduced at the games in Sydney, Australia, in 2000. Women compete in seven classes, ranging from featherweight at 109 lb (48 kg) to superheavyweight at more than 165 lb (75 kg).

Olympic weightlifters are judged on their performance of two types of lifts—the snatch and the clean and jerk. The snatch is the more difficult lift. The athlete must lift the weight off the floor and over his or her head in one flowing motion. In a move that requires quickness, balance, and strength, the lifter grabs the bar between the weights and pulls up. He then quickly squats beneath the bar. While holding the bar over his head with his arms straight, the lifter stands motionless and waits for the referee to give the signal to lower the bar.

The clean and jerk is done in two parts and with more weight than the snatch. In the first part, the lifter raises the weight from the floor to shoulder height (clean). Then he thrusts the weight by pushing it straight overhead as he almost jumps into a split position, with one foot in front and the other behind. The lifter then brings his feet together and stands motionless until the referee gives the signal to lower the weight.

Three judges observe the lifts to make sure that they are done properly and that the lifter has the weight under control. A lifter makes three attempts at each type of lift. Lifters may choose the starting weight on the bar. If the lift fails, the lifter tries again. If he succeeds, he can choose how much weight to add for his next lift. A minimum of 2.5 kg (5.5 lb) must be added. The best combined total for the two types of lifts wins the gold medal. If two lifters have the same scores, the athlete with the lower body weight wins.

In the Olympics

Athletes competed at lifting heavy stones at the ancient Olympic Games. At the first modern Olympiad in 1896, the event consisted of only one weight class (superheavyweight), and athletes competed in one-hand and two-hand lifts. The one-hand lift was dropped for the 1928 Olympics in Amsterdam. With the exception of the 1900, 1908, and 1912 Olympic Games, weightlifting has been a part of the Olympic program. Before the current tie rule of awarding the lighter competitor the higher place, two gold medals were awarded for ties. This happened in 1928 and 1936 in the lightweight event.

The United States dominated the weightlifting events from 1948 through 1956. Americans earned four gold medals at each of the games in 1948, 1952, and 1956, as well as a

WEIGHTY CONTROVERSY

Accusations and disqualifications involving drug use have plagued weightlifting. Some lifters use steroids, powerful drugs that build muscle tissue quickly. The entire Bulgarian team left the 1988 Olympics after two of its lifters were found to be using steroids. Drug abuse became so serious that, after the 1988 games, officials considered dropping weightlifting as a medal sport. So far, no action has been taken.

number of silver and bronze medals. At the 1956 games in Melbourne, Australia, American bantamweight Charles Vinci—who stood only 4 feet 10 inches tall—outweighed his weight class by 1.5 pounds. After running for an hour to sweat off the extra weight, he was still 7 ounces over the limit. A haircut at the last minute did the trick, and Vinci went on to win the gold medal, a feat he repeated in 1960.

Weight affected another bantamweight competition at the 1968 games in Mexico City. Iran's Mohammed Nasiri Seresht and Hungary's Imre Földi both lifted a total of exactly 367.5 kg (810.3 lb). Seresht took the gold because he weighed 10 ounces less than Földi. The Hungarian lifter, who won the silver medal in 1964 and 1968 and the gold in 1972, is the only weightlifter to have participated in five Olympiads.

One lifter who never worried about his own weight was American Tommy Kono, who won gold medals in 1952 and 1956 and a silver in 1960, all in different weight categories. He was known to have bulked up or dieted to compete in whichever class the team needed.

The Soviet Union dominated the 1960 games in Rome, capturing five of the six gold medals, and continued its dominance through the 1970s. Vasily Alexeyev of the Soviet Union is the most famous weightlifter of all time. He won two Olympic gold medals (1972 and 1976) in the superheavyweight division, and he was the first person ever to "jerk" more than 500 pounds.

Romania and China took most of the medals in 1984, with Romania winning eight and China winning six. The Soviet weightlifters did well again in 1988, winning six gold medals. In 1992, competing as the Unified Team after the breakup of the Soviet Union, they won five gold medals. Superheavyweight Alexander Kurlovich of Belarus won gold medals in 1988 and 1992. The runner-up in Barcelona was his countryman Leonid Taranenko, who 12 years earlier had won the heavyweight gold medal at the Moscow games.

Featherweight lifter Naim Suleymanoglu is only 5 feet tall and weighs just 141 lb (64 kg), but he is so strong that he is called "Pocket Hercules." Suleymanoglu grew up in the Eastern European country of Bulgaria. At 16, he was only the second man ever to lift three times his own body weight. When the Bulgarian government began mistreating the Turks living there, Suleymanoglu defected while at a tournament in Australia in 1986. He became a citizen of Turkey and made history at the Summer Olympics in Atlanta by becoming the first lifter to win three gold medals. He won his gold medals at the 1988, 1992, and 1996 games.

Hossein Rezazadeh of Iran set two world records in the superheavyweight division at the 2000 games. Rezazadeh set a world record of 468 lb in the snatch, then lifted 573 lb on a single lift in the clean and jerk to break Weller's overall record of 1,025 lb.

Women began competing in Olympic weightlifting in 2000. Competing in the flyweight class (48 kg/105.8 lbs), Izabela Dragneva of Bulgaria won the gold medal in the first-ever Olympic weightlifting competition for women. The women from China won four of the seven gold medals—featherweight, middleweight, light heavyweight, and super-heavyweight.

Featherweight Naim Suley-manoglu is the youngest lifter ever to set a world record, which he did at 15. He is also one of only a few athletes to lift three times his own weight.

WRESTLING

Wrestling is a competition between two athletes, each trying to bring down the other—pin him to the mat—by means of different holds and throws. Wrestling is one of the oldest sports in the world, and it was one of the most popular at the ancient Olympic Games. Today's athletes compete in two styles of wrestling: freestyle and Greco-Roman.

Origin of the Sport

Many people today may think of the costumed characters that they've seen on television when they think of wrestling, but the origin of the sport goes back to ancient times. Images of wrestling appear as early as 3000 B.C. in the Nile River valley. There are also references to the sport in ancient and medieval Indian epics and hymns. Italian explorer Marco Polo tells the story of a Tartar princess who challenged her suitors to a wrestling match.

Wrestling as a competitive sport first appeared in the Olympic Games in ancient Greece around 708 B.C. The ancient Greek philosopher Plato believed that wrestling was good for building strength and maintaining health. The best-known wrestler is probably Jacob, the biblical figure in the book of Genesis, who wrestled all night with a mysterious figure thought to be God. Wrestling has been popular in Great Britain for centuries, and Irish immigrants probably brought the sport to the United States. The young Abraham Lincoln was known to have wrestled. During the Civil War, soldiers engaged in wrestling matches for exercise and entertainment.

The Amateur Athletic Union organized the first freestyle wrestling tournament in the United States in 1888. The first modern Olympics in 1896 featured a single bout of heavyweight Greco-Roman wrestling. Freestyle wrestling became part of the Olympics in 1904. The sport's main governing body, the International Amateur Wrestling Federation (FILA), was formed in 1912 at the Olympic Games in Antwerp, Belgium. The U.S. Wrestling Federation, created in 1969, became the governing body of the sport in the United States.

Fast Facts

First Olympic competition

Athens, Greece; 1896

Legendary athletes

Ivar Johansson, **Sweden**

Aleksandr Karelin, **Soviet Union**

Aleksandr Medved, **Soviet Union**

Carl Westergren, **Sweden**

Criteria for winning

Most points scored

Competing in the Event

Olympic wrestling is for men only. Athletes compete in eight weight classes, ranging from flyweight (119 pounds, or 54 kilograms) to superheavyweight (286 lb, or 130 kg). They wear a tight-fitting bodysuit, called a singlet, which enables them to move freely. Wrestlers compete on a circular mat, and matches consist of two 3-minute periods.

Wrestling matches begin with both athletes standing on their feet and facing each other on the mat. At the referee's signal, the wrestlers grab each other in a tie-up. A contestant wins by pinning his opponent, by scoring the most points, or by building up a 10-point lead. Wrestlers receive points for takedowns, near falls, reversals, rides, and escapes. A wrestler can also earn points when his opponent commits a penalty.

In both freestyle and Greco-Roman contests, a wrestler's objective is to pin his opponent to the mat. The main difference between the two styles is that Greco-Roman wrestlers may not hold their opponents below the waist or use their legs in an aggressive manner to take down an opponent. As the name implies, freestyle wrestlers are less restricted in the types of moves they are allowed to make. They may use their legs to grab their opponent's limbs or torso and hold or pin an opponent. Tripping or tackling by using one's legs are also allowed in freestyle wrestling.

Bringing an opponent to the mat is called a takedown and is worth one point. If the downed wrestler rises, he is awarded one point for an escape. A wrestler can control how his opponent moves by holding his arm and leg in a hold called a ride. A reversal occurs when a wrestler goes from a defensive position (beneath his opponent) to an offensive position (on top of his opponent). A near fall happens when a wrestler almost pins his opponent. To successfully complete a fall for a pin, a wrestler must keep his opponent's shoulder blades on the mat for half a second. Throwing an opponent from a standing position onto his back is worth five points. If the score is tied, officials call a 3-minute overtime period. If neither wrestler has scored by the end of the overtime period, the referee, the judge, and the mat chairman choose the winner by majority vote.

POLITICAL PROTEST

At the 1996 Summer Olympics in Atlanta, Georgia, Elmadi Jabrailov of Kazakhstan faced Tucuman Jabrailov of Moldova for the freestyle middleweight gold medal. The brothers, who were from Chechnya, had chosen not to represent Russia because of its war against the people of Chechnya.

In the Olympics

Although wrestling was included in the first modern-day Olympic Games, the sport was left out of the 1900 games. Wrestling came back in 1904, when athletes competed in seven weight classes of freestyle events. Greco-Roman wrestling was introduced at the 1908 games in London with competitions in four weight classes.

By 1912, at the games in Stockholm, Sweden, freestyle competition had been dropped in favor of Greco-Roman wrestling. The popularity of Greco-Roman wrestling in the Scandinavian countries was apparent when Finland claimed three gold medals and Sweden one. In a spectacularly long light-heavyweight match, Sweden's Anders Ahlgren and Finland's Ivar Böhling struggled for 9 hours before officials called the contest a draw and awarded both men silver medals. As if 9 hours weren't long enough, the longest match in Olympic history also occurred that year. In the middleweight class, Russian wrestler Martin Klein and Finland's Alfred Asikainen battled it out for 11 hours and 40 minutes, until Klein finally pinned Asikainen for the silver medal. Sweden's Claes Johanson won the gold medal by default because Klein, not surprisingly, was too tired to compete in the final match.

Sweden's Carl Westergren earned the first of his three gold medals at the 1920 games in Antwerp, Belgium. Only three other wrestlers—Sweden's Ivar Johansson and the Soviet Union's Aleksandr Medved and Aleksandr Karelin—have won three golds. Westergren, who is considered the inventor of the forward takedown, won his medals in three different divisions. He earned his 1920 medal competing as a middleweight, then bulked up to win the light-heavyweight medal in 1924, and finally won the heavyweight medal in 1932.

Sweden's Ivar Johansson won his first two gold medals at the 1932 games. After wining the freestyle middleweight medal, he spent the next 24 hours sweating and fasting to lose enough weight to compete in the Greco-Roman welterweight competition. He lost 11 pounds and then won four more matches and a second gold medal. Four years later, he successfully defended his Greco-Roman middleweight title.

Turkey dominated the freestyle events at the 1948 games in London, winning six medals, while Sweden went home with seven in the Greco-Roman events. Soviet wrestlers made their debut in 1952 and enjoyed both good luck and good timing.

The Soviet team dominated the 1968 games and became an even stronger force in 1972, capturing a total of nine gold and four silver medals. When he claimed his third gold medal, Soviet superheavyweight freestyler Aleksandr Medved became the first wrestler to win gold medals in three consecutive Olympiads.

Bruce Baumgartner is probably America's most successful Greco-Roman wrestler. The superheavyweight won the gold medal in 1984 and finished in second place in 1988. In 1992, after a disappointing year, Baumgartner came roaring back to retake the Olympic championship. He outscored five of his six opponents by a combined total score of 35-1 and threw his sixth opponent in only 11 seconds. In 1996, he won a bronze, his fourth Olympic medal.

Russia's Aleksandr Karelin became the first wrestler to win the same weight division three times in a row (1988, 1992, and 1996). Karelin, who is called "The Siberian Bear," is known for his awesome reverse body lift. When an opponent is lying on his stomach, Karelin grabs him around the waist, lifts him off the mat, and flips him onto his back before pinning him to the mat. In a stunning upset at the Sydney games in 2000, Rulon Gardner of the United States defeated the previously unbeaten Russian in his bid for four straight Olympic gold medals.

Kevin Bracken of the U.S. (in blue) attempts to gain a point with a takedown by throwing Varteres Samourgachev of Russia during the men's quarterfinals in Sydney.

Abebe Bikila
marathon runner

Abebe Bikila, from Ethiopia, stunned the running world when he won the marathon at the Olympic Games in 1960. Competing for the first time outside his hometown of Addis Ababa, Bikila ran the 26 miles barefoot over the cobblestone streets of Rome. Not only did he run without shoes, but he also logged the best time ever for the event— 2 hours, 15 minutes, and 16.2 seconds!

Bikila was born on August 7, 1932. A man of strong principles, Bikila believed that amateur athletes should not give endorsements and should not be paid to advertise products. Like the ancient Greeks, Bikila believed that sports and politics should be kept separate. As he once said, "Sport is for international friendship. The Olympics have nothing to do with war—not with any war."

Shortly after the 1960 Olympic marathon began, Bikila and Rhadi Ben Abdesselem of Morocco pulled ahead of the rest. They ran side by side for miles, never looking at each other, along a route lined by thousands of spectators. About a mile from the finish line stood the obelisk of Axum, an Ethiopian monument that Italian troops had taken in the 1930s. Just as Bikila was passing the obelisk, he made his move. Pulling away from Rhadi, he increased his lead by 200 yards to break through the tape at the finish line, beating Emil Zátopek's Olympic record by nearly 8 minutes.

Bikila ran the marathon again at the 1964 games in Tokyo, Japan. Just 40 days before the games, he had undergone surgery to remove his appendix. Even so, he beat his own Olympic record by 4 minutes and 5 seconds.

Bikila attempted to win the marathon a third time in Mexico City in 1968, but he had to drop out after 17 kilometers because of a broken bone in his leg. The following year, in 1969, a terrible car crash left him paralyzed from the waist down. He died in 1973 at the age of 41. Once asked how he was able to face life in a wheelchair, this deeply religious man replied, "I was overjoyed when I won the marathon twice. But I accepted those victories as I accept this tragedy. I have to accept both circumstances as facts of life and live happily."

Running more than 26 miles barefoot, Abebe Bikila wins the gold for the marathon and sets a new Olympic record.

Fanny Blankers-Koen
sprinter and hurdler

At the 1948 Olympics in London, England, Fanny Blankers-Koen did something no other woman has ever done. She captured four track-and-field gold medals at a single Olympiad—for the 100 meters, the 200 meters, the 80-meter hurdles, and the 4×100-meter relay. She might have won two additional medals, but at the time athletes could compete in only four events. Blankers-Koen chose not to enter two events for which she already held world records—the high jump and the long jump.

Koen came by her athletic ability naturally. Born into a family of athletes, Koen joined a local sports club when she was only six. She became an excellent swimmer and runner. At 16, she joined the Amsterdam Dames' Athletic Club and traveled to the city twice a week to train with some of the best track athletes in the country. At one of her first track meets, she met Jan Blankers, a track coach. He saw her potential as a jumper and sprinter. At his insistence, Koen was invited to join the Dutch team for the 1936 Olympic Games in Berlin. The couple later married in 1940.

After a disappointing performance in Berlin, Blankers-Koen had to sit out the games of 1940 and 1944, which were canceled because World War II raged in Europe. Finally, when she was 30 years old and the mother of three, Blankers-Koen had the opportunity to compete in the 1948 games in London.

Fanny Blankers-Koen (far right) won the 80-meter hurdles, setting an Olympic record. By the end of the 1948 games in London, she had captured the gold in four events.

Everyone assumed she was too old to do well in the sprint races. Furthermore, many people disapproved of her involvement in sports. They believed that sports took time away from her responsibilities as a wife and a mother. A photograph in a Dutch newspaper showed her practicing the high jump while her children played nearby.

Blankers-Koen had waited a long time to compete for the gold, however, and she was determined to do so. Leaving the children with her father in Amsterdam, Blankers-Koen and her husband left for London. Her first event, the 100-meter dash, was run in a driving rainstorm. Racing through the mud, she won the contest by 3 yards and in record time—11.9 seconds.

Blankers-Koen got off to a poor start in the 80-meter hurdles. She caught up to the British favorite, Maureen Gardner, at the second hurdle. Then she took the fifth hurdle slightly late, hit the top bar, and stumbled to the finish line. Before anyone knew who had won the race, the band began to play "God Save the King." When she heard the British national anthem, Blankers-Koen believed she had lost. As it turned out, the band played the song because the British royal family had just entered the stadium. Moments later, the results appeared on the scoreboard, declaring Blankers-Koen the winner in 11.2 seconds, another Olympic record.

The pressure to win a third gold medal was great. Prior to the semifinals for the 200-meter race, Blankers-Koen told her husband that she wanted to go home. He replied, "If you don't want to go on, you must not. But I'm afraid you will be sorry later if you don't run." Recovering her strength and determination, Blankers-Koen won her third gold medal, by a margin of 7 yards—the greatest margin of victory ever in a women's Olympic 200-meters. The next day she anchored Holland's 4×100-meter relay team. The Dutch team was 5 yards behind and in fourth place when Blankers-Koen took the baton. She overcame this deficit and brought her team to an amazing victory.

During her long career, Blankers-Koen won four Olympic gold medals and five European championships. She also played a major role in popularizing women's sports after World War II. In 1948, the Associated Press selected her Female Athlete of the Year. She was inducted into the Women's Sports Hall of Fame in 1980.

Nadia Comaneci
gymnast

In 1976, at the Olympic Games in Montreal, Canada, 14-year-old Nadia Comaneci of Romania became the first gymnast ever to receive a perfect score of ten. Even more remarkable is that by the end of that Olympiad, Comaneci had earned a total of seven perfect scores.

Comaneci was born in the small industrial town of Onesti, Romania, in 1961. When she was only five years old, the now-famous gymnastics coach Bela Karolyi spotted her and a friend doing acrobatics in the kindergarten playground. When Comaneci disappeared into her classroom after the bell rang, Karolyi searched the school for her, asking the girls in each class, "Who loves gymnastics?" until he found Nadia, who jumped up shouting "I do, I do!" Young Comaneci was then enrolled in the sports school where she began her training. Karolyi said of his special student, "She is intelligent, dedicated, loves the sport, and has a strong spirit; she knows no fear."

Nadia Comaneci performs a back handspring on the balance beam, her strongest event, at the 1976 games in Montreal.

ESCAPE TO FREEDOM

What first seemed like a palace turned into a prison after Comaneci was denied permission to leave Romania. Comaneci described her escape from Romania to a London newspaper. "It was midnight when we started walking through mud and open countryside," she told the reporter. "We were stumbling. Often we crawled through water and ice." It took the group six hours to walk the last ten miles to the Hungarian border.

From early on, Comaneci demonstrated her talent and competitiveness. In 1971, at the age of nine, she became Romania's junior champion. Two years later, she became national champion. At 13 she defeated her idol, the five-time European champion Lyudmilla Turischeva of the Soviet Union, to become the youngest gymnast ever to win the European championship. Finally, at the 1976 Olympics, she captured the attention of the sports world, earning five Olympic medals: three gold, a silver, and a bronze. Her extraordinary performances put gymnastics front and center on the prime-time television schedule.

At the 1980 games, Comaneci was close to winning her second gold medal in the all-around competition but was behind by a small margin. She needed to score 9.95 on her final event, the balance beam, in order to win. The balance beam was Comaneci's strongest event. Her performance this time was nearly perfect. After a long debate over her score, the judges awarded Comaneci a 9.85, thus giving the gold medal to the Soviet gymnast. The following day, Comaneci won gold medals in the individual balance beam and floor exercise.

Romania honored the young gymnast in several ways. She was the youngest person ever to receive the Hero of Socialist Labor award, the highest honor in her country. Comaneci lived in a large house and drove a car with a special license plate that gave her the status of a top party official with the right to park anywhere. "She is the most famous of all Romanians," said a commentator. "Probably not even Dracula is as famous." But Romania, under the leadership of dictator Nicolae Ceausescu, was becoming a harsh place. When Comaneci was invited to be an honored guest at the 1988 Olympic Games in Seoul, South Korea, Ceausescu refused to let her go.

Comaneci finally rebelled. Following the example of her coach, who had defected to the United States in 1981, she and six others slipped across the border to Hungary in the middle of the night on November 27, 1989. Four days later, she arrived in New York City with a new, positive outlook. Comaneci came to the United States with a goal to coach and to encourage future American gymnasts. She began teaching at the Bart Conner Gymnastics Academy. Conner, also an Olympic champion, and Nadia Comaneci found much to share besides their love for gymnastics. The two married in 1996.

Mildred "Babe" Didrikson
track and field

When Babe Didrikson arrived in Los Angeles for the 1932 Olympics, she boasted that she would "beat everybody in sight." Her bragging may have angered some of her teammates, but it was more than just empty talk. At the Olympic trials, Didrikson, who was 18, had qualified to compete in all five individual women's track-and-field events, but the rules allowed her to enter only three events. She chose the 80-meter hurdles, javelin throw, and high jump.

Didrikson captured the gold in the first two events. Although she tied for first place in the high jump, she was awarded the silver medal because she jumped over the bar headfirst, which in those days was illegal. As it turned out, Didrikson was ahead of her time. Today, all high jumpers use the headfirst style of high jumping.

Born in 1911 in Port Arthur, Texas, Mildred Ella Didrikson was the sixth of seven children. Her parents, Ole and Hannah Didriksen, were Norwegian immigrants. (Didrikson changed the spelling of her name later in life.) Interested in sports from an early age, Didrikson excelled at every game. Her ability to hit home runs like the famous Yankee ballplayer Babe Ruth earned her the nickname "Babe." In addition to her skills with a bat, she could kick a football farther and throw a baseball harder than any of the boys who played in her neighborhood. She learned to play basketball in elementary school. In high school, Didrikson played on every team open to girls.

Didrikson left high school to take a job in a Dallas insurance company that had an amateur basketball team. The team was called the Golden Cyclones. Although she was paid to type, her real job was to play basketball. She led the team to two finals and one national championship, scoring an amazing 106 points in one game. Didrikson was the insurance company's sole representative at the 1932 Amateur

Babe Didrikson rears back for a throw at the 1932 games in Los Angeles. She captured the gold in the javelin competition, setting an Olympic women's record of 143 feet 4 inches.

HAPPIEST WHEN PLAYING SPORTS

Babe Didrikson was a born athlete and was probably happiest when she was out on the playing field. Her friend and colleague Patty Berg once said, "Sometimes I find myself leaning back in a chair thinking about Babe and I have to smile. She was the happiest girl you ever saw, like a kid."

Athletic Union's track-and-field championships. She won the team competition—scoring 30 points, eight more than the entire second-place team! That same year, she distinguished herself at the Olympic Games by winning individual medals in running, throwing, and jumping events. Grantland Rice, the leading sportswriter of the day, wrote, "She is beyond all belief until you see her perform. Then you finally understand that you are looking at the most flawless section of muscle harmony, of complete mental and physical coordination the world of sports has ever seen."

After her Olympic success, Didrikson turned professional. She founded and played on the Babe Didrikson All-Star Basketball Team. She traveled throughout the country pitching for the House of David all-male exhibition baseball team. Didrikson pitched for several major league teams in exhibition games, once even striking out the legendary Joe DiMaggio. As much an entertainer as an athlete, Didrikson drew crowds wherever she went. More interested in making sports history than making money, Didrikson became a champion golfer. Golf was one of only a few sports deemed acceptable for women athletes, and Didrikson decided she would excel at it. Between 1935 and 1954, she won 82 amateur and professional tournaments, including an astounding 17 in a row. In 1938, Didrikson met and married wrestler George Zaharias.

In 1947, Babe Didrikson Zaharias became the first American woman to win the British Women's Amateur title. In 1950, she co-founded the Ladies Professional Golf Association (LPGA) with Patty Berg. That same year, Associated Press sportswriters voted her the greatest female athlete of the first half of the 20th century. This was not the first time the Associated Press recognized Didrikson's talent. They voted her Athlete of the Year six times throughout her life, once for her accomplishments in track and field and five more times for her outstanding records in golf.

In 1953, Didrikson's life took a tragic turn when she underwent cancer surgery. Courageous and remarkable as always, she was back on the golf course the following year, winning the U.S. Women's Open championship by an unheard-of 12 strokes. In 1956, the cancer returned, and Babe Didrikson Zaharias died at the age of 45.

Teresa Edwards
basketball player

Teresa Edwards transformed women's basketball and helped its development as a professional sport. At 36, when she returned to her fifth Olympic Games, she was one of only 17 athletes ever to be chosen for five U.S. Olympic teams. She was also one of ten athletes to ever compete in five Olympiads.

Born in 1964 in Cairo, Georgia, Edwards grew up playing sports with the boys in her neighborhood. She played softball and football on the street behind her house and shot baskets through an old bicycle rim nailed to a tree in the front yard. The hours of practice and pickup games in the park paid off when Edwards made the seventh-grade team at Washington Middle School.

Edwards attended the University of Georgia, where she was an All-America point guard in 1985 and 1986. During

Teresa Edwards dribbles the ball during the game against Japan at the 1996 Olympics in Atlanta.

BORN TO PLAY BASKETBALL

Teresa Edwards was only 17 years old when she first donned the red-white-and-blue uniform of the U.S. women's team. During her long career, Edwards had represented her nation 204 times on 18 different national teams that won a total of 14 gold medals, 1 silver medal, and 3 bronze medals. "I was born to play basketball," she once said. "It's been my life's joy. If anything bothered me, I'd head to the gym and dribble it off. Basketball has always been my escape."

her college career, she led Georgia to a 116-17 record. After college, Edwards turned professional, playing in Italy for two seasons and in Japan for three. Hours of practice left little time for other activities. She later recalled that the experience made her a better player and "mentally tough." Edwards was just 20 when she played in her first Olympics. The last player off the bench, Edwards watched most of the tournament as the U.S. women's team won all six games and the gold medal.

By 1988, Edwards had transformed herself from observer to star of the American team. As point guard and the team's best ball handler, Edwards ran the offense and averaged more than 16 points per game. In the gold medal game against Yugoslavia, she scored 18 points. The United States won 77-70, and Edwards took home her second gold medal.

The U.S. women's team had become an international powerhouse, winning 42 consecutive games in international competition between 1982 and 1991. At the 1992 games in Barcelona, the squad looked to be at the top of its game. In the semifinal game, however, the Unified Team (composed of athletes from the former Soviet Union) upset the favored Americans 79-73. The United States bounced back to beat Cuba for the bronze medal, but bitter defeat by the Unified Team was hard to swallow.

To prepare for the 1996 Olympics, the United States formed a permanent national team in 1995 and promptly accumulated 52 straight victories. The U.S. women's team regained the title with a crushing 111-87 triumph over Brazil. Playing in her fourth Olympiad, Edwards averaged eight assists per game. In the eight games of the tournament, no team came close to beating Edwards and her teammates.

Edwards was 36 when the 2000 games began in Sydney, Australia. It would be her fifth and last Olympiad, and she could still control a game like no other player. A starter in all eight games of the tournament, Edwards played 29 of the 40 minutes of her last game, scored six points, and had three assists. The U.S. team beat Australia 76-54, and Edwards left the court with her fourth gold medal. She was the last player off the court following the medal ceremony. Slowly walking to the midcourt circle, Edwards thought about her basketball career and began to cry. She knew it was time to retire.

Kornelia Ender
swimmer

In 1972, when Kornelia Ender was only 13, she won three silver medals at the Olympic Games in Munich, Germany. Four years later, in Montreal, the women on the East German swim team won 11 gold medals in 13 events, while setting five world records and establishing themselves as the fastest female team in the world. Ender was the best one of all.

Kornelia Ender was born in 1958 in Plauen, East Germany (now Germany). She had always been a fast swimmer. When Ender was only six years old, she attracted the attention of the East German government. She was sent to a special sports school to develop her talent for swimming.

The training schedule was tough. Ender trained six days a week, swimming as much as eight miles a day. She later recalled, "There were times when, honestly, I felt I'd had enough of training. But I never seriously thought of giving up."

The rigorous training paid off. A year after her promising debut at the Munich games, Ender broke the world record for the 100-meter freestyle. This was the first of the 23 world records she set in individual events during her extraordinary swimming career.

Suspected drug use led to accusations that the East German women had used anabolic steroids. These illegal drugs are known for building size and strength, and many athletes use them in spite of their terrible side effects. In the early 1970s, state-owned drug companies in East Germany were working with coaches to develop a generation of superathletes. Ender recalls being given a "cocktail of vitamins" after every workout to help her muscles recover faster. In 1991, West and East Germany were reunited, and the East German sports program was disbanded. Later that year, East German swimming officials admitted to injecting their athletes with steroids without their knowledge or consent.

Whether they were the result of steroids or of sheer athletic ability, Ender's achievements were remarkable. In 1976, she won two gold medals a mere 27 minutes apart, a feat regarded by many as the greatest sports achievement ever. She was also the first female swimmer to win four gold medals in a single Olympiad.

East Germany's Kornelia Ender waves to the crowd from the victory platform after winning the women's 200-meter freestyle event at the 1976 games in Montreal.

Ray Ewry
standing jumper

Although Ray Ewry won more Olympic medals than any other athlete, he is virtually unknown because the events in which he competed have been discontinued. Ewry won a total of ten gold medals in the Olympic Games of 1900, 1904, 1908, and the Intercalated (Interim) Games of 1906.

Born in 1873, in Lafayette, Indiana, Ewry had polio as a young boy. Although his doctors expected that he might never walk, young Ewry began exercising with fierce determination. He eventually regained the use of his legs and added jumping exercises to strengthen his muscles. By the time he enrolled at Purdue University, he had become a superb athlete.

After college, Ewry moved to New York City. As a member of the prestigious New York Athletic Club, Ewry participated in the 1900 Olympics in Paris. Ewry's events were among the most difficult. Without the momentum of a running start, standing jumpers had only the strength of their leg muscles to launch them into the air. At the Paris games, competitors had to overcome the additional challenge of poor field conditions. French officials had refused to install a cinder track at the park where the events were held, leaving the athletes to launch themselves from the heavily watered grassy surface.

Despite these difficulties, Ewry won three gold medals. First, he set a world record in the standing high jump, with a clearance of 5 feet 5 inches (1.655 meters). Next, he produced a standing long jump of 10 ft 10 in (3.30 m). Finally, he made a standing triple jump of 34 ft 8.5 in (10.58 m). One day, three events, three gold medals—an Olympic achievement that has never been matched.

Ray Ewry took three gold medals at the 1904 games and two each at the 1906 and 1908 Olympiads. He had entered ten events, winning a gold medal each time.

He retired as the undefeated Olympic champion of standing jumpers. Standing jumps were eliminated shortly thereafter, which means that Ewry's Olympic records will stand forever.

Although stricken with polio as a child, Ray Ewry captured the gold in the standing high jump event at the 1908 games. By the end of the games, Ewry had a career total of ten gold medals.

Sylvie Frechette
synchronized swimmer

Sylvie Frechette of Canada won a gold medal in synchronized swimming at the 1992 Barcelona games. She had to wait more than a year, however, to receive her gold medal. A judging error at the Olympics almost cost Frechette the solo title she had worked so hard to achieve.

Born in Montreal, Canada, on June 27, 1967, Frechette became interested in synchronized swimming soon after it was introduced to the Olympics in 1984. She was attracted to the elegance, beauty, and artistry of the sport. From 1988 until the Barcelona Olympiad, she finished first in all but one of the international competitions she entered.

Frechette performed original solo routines and set high standards for her sport. At the 1991 World Aquatic Games in Australia, she amazed the judges and spectators by scoring seven perfect scores of ten. In 1992, however, Frechette went to the Olympics carrying much more than the pressure of being the world champion. A week before the opening ceremonies of the Barcelona Olympiad, she returned home from a day of training to find the body of her boyfriend and business manager, who apparently had taken his own life. After the initial shock, Frechette put aside her grief and flew to Barcelona, determined to compete. "I know this is what he wants," she said. "He knew how much the Olympics meant to me."

Frechette's chief rival in the Olympic solo event was Kristen Babb-Sprague of the United States. The competition consisted of the compulsory figures (in which each swimmer performs four required movements) and the free routine. Frechette was strong in figures and hoped to build a large

Sylvie Frechette waves to the crowd after placing second in the solo synchronized swimming competition at the 1992 games.

lead over Babb-Sprague, who was expected to do better in the free routine. After performing the final required move, an albatross, Frechette received marks between 9.2 and 9.6 from four of the five judges. The Brazilian judge accidentally punched in 8.7 on her computer. The judge realized her mistake and tried to change it to 9.7, the score she had intended. There was a delay as the judge tried to correct her mistake, and the bad mark wound up being counted in the final score.

Canadian officials pleaded Frechette's case, but to no avail. The score had already been displayed to the public as the official score, and IOC rules stated that once a score was posted, it could not be changed. Frechette later won the free routine, but without enough points to offset the effect of the error in the score for the albatross. Sadly, Frechette lost the gold medal by a tiny margin—a little more than a tenth of a point.

The outpouring of sympathy for Frechette's losses, both athletic and personal, helped her face the enormous disappointment at the Olympics and go on with her life. Then, 16 months later, the IOC decided to review the incident and presented Frechette with her gold medal, declaring her and Babb-Sprague co-medalists. "I wanted that gold medal," Frechette admitted, "but I received so much more from people than I ever expected. Not materially, but emotionally."

After nearly two years of retirement from the sport, Frechette (by then 29) began to train for the Canadian team for the 1996 games in Atlanta. The solo competition had been replaced with a team competition. As a member of the Canadian team, Frechette won the silver medal in Atlanta. "In Barcelona, I was alone," she said. "Here, we're ten athletes. I feel pride. Pride in the way we swam in the pool and proud to have a silver medal around my neck."

Frechette's talent at synchronized swimming and her ability to handle intense personal tragedy with courage and dignity earned her professional honors and the admiration of many fans. She was voted Female Athlete of the Year four times in a row, 1989 through 1992, by the Aquatic Federation of Canada. In 1999, Frechette was inducted into Canada's Sports Hall of Fame.

Jackie Joyner-Kersee
heptathlete and long jumper

Jackie Joyner-Kersee exemplifies what talent, hard work, and determination can do. Described by many as the greatest female athlete of the last 50 years, Joyner-Kersee overcame serious obstacles to realize her dream of competing in the Olympic Games. She not only competed in one of the toughest events—the heptathlon—but she also became one of the highest scorers ever, breaking world records and some of her own along the way.

Jacqueline Joyner was born in 1962 in East St. Louis, Illinois, a town on the banks of the Mississippi River. When the Joyners named their infant daughter for the wife of President John F. Kennedy, her grandmother declared, "Someday this girl will be the first lady of something." That "something" turned out to be athletics.

Joyner became interested in sports at the Mayor Brown Youth Center near her home. Although she came in last in her first race, she was not discouraged. When she was 12, Joyner could jump distances of over 17 feet (5.2 meters). At 14, Joyner began to focus on the five-event pentathlon and declared to family and friends her intention to one day compete in the Olympics.

Joyner was a three-sport athlete in high school. She played basketball and volleyball and set a record for the long jump. Joyner graduated in the top 10 percent of her high school class and chose to attend the University of California at Los Angeles on a basketball scholarship. In 1981, track coach Bob Kersee observed Joyner's natural athletic ability and her explosive speed and urged her to train for the heptathlon.

Joyner won two National Collegiate Athletic Association heptathlon titles and a silver medal in the event at the

Jackie Joyner-Kersee leaps through the air to win the gold and set a new Olympic record in the long jump at the 1988 games in Seoul.

HONORS GALORE

Jackie Joyner-Kersee has received numerous honors and awards. Among them are the following:

Sullivan Award (1986)

Jesse Owens Award (1986, 1987)

Track & Field News Athlete of the Year (1986, 1987, 1994)

U.S. Olympic Committee Sportswoman of the Year (1986, 1987)

Associated Press Female Athlete of the Year (1987)

Women's Sports Foundation Flo Hyman Award (1987)

Women's Sports Foundation Sportswoman of the Year (1992)

1984 Olympics. Competing with a painful hamstring injury, Joyner lost to Glynis Nunn of Australia by only five points (less than 0.4 second) in the 800-meter run. In 1986, after graduating from college, Joyner married Bob Kersee. At the Goodwill Games that same year, Joyner-Kersee became the first woman to score more than 7,000 points in the heptathlon. She had achieved personal bests in every event, and her score of 7,148 shattered the world record by 200 points. Less than a month later, she broke her own record with a score of 7,161.

At the 1988 Olympics Games in Seoul, South Korea, Jackie Joyner-Kersee trounced her closest competitor by nearly 400 points. In doing so, she set a new world record with 7,291 points and won her first gold medal. Only five days later, she captured the gold medal in the long jump and became the first American woman ever to win that event.

Joyner-Kersee successfully defended her heptathlon title at the 1992 games in Barcelona, Spain, making her the only woman to win back-to-back heptathlon gold medals. At the 1996 games in Atlanta, Joyner-Kersee's dream of a heptathlon "three-peat" was thwarted when a sore leg forced her to withdraw from the competition. Never a quitter, however, she went on to win a bronze in the long jump despite her injury. Entering the final round in seventh place, the 34-year-old champion knew she had one great jump left inside her. Sure enough, Joyner-Kersee leaped 22 feet 11.5 inches (7.0 meters) to catapult into third place for the bronze.

Joyner-Kersee retired from Olympic track and field as a member of four U.S. Olympic teams—1984, 1988, 1992, and 1996—and a winner of three gold medals, one silver, and two bronze. Recalling her own beginnings, she remains committed to her community by promoting physical fitness among young people, especially in cities where opportunities are limited. In a 1993 interview for *Women's Sports & Fitness,* Joyner-Kersee was asked about her unusually long athletic career. She replied, "A lot of it has to do with how you take care of your body while you're young, and I've always taken care of myself." Good advice from one who knows.

Kip Keino
runner

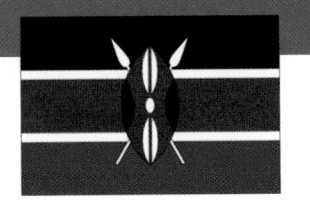

Today many of the world's best distance runners come from Africa. The reason for this may be that in the 1960s and 1970s, many young people wanted to be just like Kip Keino, one of the first great runners to come from the African continent. Keino was born in 1940 on a farm about 240 miles from Nairobi, the capital of Kenya. He trained mostly in the mountains, about 6,000 feet above sea level. At such high altitudes, the body has to work harder because there is less oxygen, and this helped Keino become an exceptionally strong runner.

Keino's mother died when he was only two. Raised by his grandmother and educated at a missionary school, Keino left his farming village at age 18 to become a police officer and a cross-country runner. At 22, Keino joined the Kenyan team that traveled to Australia for the Commonwealth Games. This was to be his first trip abroad.

By 1965, Keino had become a real crowd pleaser. Running with a long, easy stride, he typically wore a bright orange cap pulled down to his ears. As he neared the end of the race, Keino would joyously fling off his cap and sprint to the finish line.

At the 1968 games in Mexico City, Kip Keino (right) is all smiles after his gold medal finish in the 1,500-meter race—an event he almost missed.

MORE THAN A GREAT RUNNER

In addition to being a great runner, Kip Keino is also a terrific person. During his time at the police academy, Keino found three homeless, starving children wandering alone near Kenya's northern border. He took the children home, where he and his wife Phyllis fed and clothed them. Since that time, the Keinos have taken in more than 100 orphans. Most of the time they and the children live on the Keinos' 190-acre farm in Kenya's western highlands. Although the Keinos also operate a sporting goods store, the farm and its shifting population of homeless children have been the center of Kip Keino's world.

The 1968 Olympics took place in Mexico City, which is about 7,200 feet above sea level. Keino, who was then 28 and used to training at high altitude, was considered a favorite. Then, just before the races began, he became ill with a gallbladder infection. Despite severe abdominal pain, Keino went ahead with his plans to run in the 10,000-meter race. He was in the lead with several other runners, with only two laps to go, when the pain became so intense that he fell to the ground in agony. With the doctor's help, he rose to his feet and finished the race, even though he had been disqualified. Four days later, he took second place in the 5,000-meter run, losing by just 0.02 second—and about 4 feet—to Tunisia's Mohamed Gammoudi.

On the day of the 1,500-meter race, Keino was resting, on doctor's orders, instead of preparing for the race with the other athletes. But as race time drew near, Keino could rest no longer. He quickly set off for the stadium, only to find himself in a terrible traffic jam. He could not risk being late for the race, so he got out of the car and jogged the last mile to the Olympic stadium. His rival was American Jim Ryun, unbeaten for over three years and holder of the world record for the 1,500-m race. Because Keino had never been able to outrun Ryun, he decided to change his strategy for this race. He hoped to build a huge lead early in the race, making Ryun's sprint at the end just a meaningless dash.

Keino believed this was the race of his life. He would later recall thinking, "If I die, I die here." After two laps, Keino took the lead and pulled away from the pack. The other runners waited for him to tire, but he never did. Ryun's famous finishing sprint was not enough, and the Kenyan runner won by 20 m, the largest margin of victory in the history of the 1,500-m event at the Olympics.

At the 1972 games in Munich, Germany, Keino finished second in the 1,500 meters and won the gold medal in the 3,000-m steeplechase. With very little hurdling experience, he had entered the steeplechase as a challenge. Although his lack of experience caused him to jump "like an animal," Kip outleaped his teammate Ben Jipcho. "I had a lot of fun jumping the hurdles," he said later. In 1987, *Sports Illustrated* selected Keino Sportsman of the Year, as much for his work off the track as for his skill and sportsmanship on it.

Greg Louganis
diver

Arguably the finest diver ever, Greg Louganis of the United States became the only man to sweep both the platform and the springboard diving events in back-to-back Olympic Games. In addition, he won 5 world championships, held 47 national championship titles, and earned 6 gold medals at the Pan American Games. At 5 feet 9 inches (1.75 meters) and 168 pounds (76.27 kilograms), he displayed the acrobatic grace and muscular flexibility of a ballet dancer. Louganis, who once described himself as a panther, was also a fierce competitor.

Adopted when he was only nine months old, Louganis grew up in El Cajon, California. Classmates teased him because of his dark skin and his inability to read. Louganis had dyslexia, a learning disability that makes reading difficult. The young boy found an escape in diving. "The pool was my sanctuary," he later recalled.

When Louganis was 11, he competed at the Junior Olympics, scoring a perfect 10. He impressed Dr. Sammy Lee, the platform diving champion of the 1948 and 1952 Olympic Games. "When I first watched him," said Dr. Lee, "I said to myself, 'My god, that's the greatest talent I've ever seen!'" In 1975, Lee agreed to coach Louganis.

Olympic success began for Louganis the following year. He was performing in the 10-m platform event at the 1976 games in Montreal, Canada. Although he was a newcomer to international diving, Louganis was leading the legendary Klaus Dibiasi of Italy midway through the competition. The Italian, a platform specialist, had won gold medals at both the 1968 and 1972 games. Dibiasi eventually took the lead and held on to win his third consecutive gold medal. Louganis, awarded the silver medal, had nearly pulled off one of the most remarkable upsets in Olympic diving history.

The U.S. team boycotted the Moscow games in 1980 to protest the Soviet invasion of Afghanistan. In 1984, Louganis was back and performing brilliantly. As the overwhelming favorite, he easily captured the gold medal for the springboard event. He executed a near-perfect reverse tuck and earned another gold medal, becoming the first man since

Greg Louganis performs a dive at the 1984 games in Los Angeles, where he won both the springboard and platform events by phenomenal margins over his nearest competitor.

PERFECT TEN BY SEVEN

Many people think Greg Louganis was the best diver ever. Certainly the judges at the 1982 World Championships thought so. At that competition, Louganis became the first diver at an international meet to receive a perfect score of 10 from all seven judges.

In 1985, Louganis was inducted into the United States Olympic Hall of Fame.

1928 to win both the springboard and the platform events at the same Olympiad. Louganis was the undisputed king of diving. His winning margins—94 points in the springboard, 67 in the platform—were astounding accomplishments in a sport that regards a 10-point victory as good and 20 points as an absolute clobbering. For his outstanding achievements at the Los Angeles games, Louganis was honored with the James E. Sullivan Award. This mark of distinction is given annually by the Amateur Athletic Union to the athlete "who has done the most during the year to advance the cause of sportsmanship."

Many people thought Louganis would retire after the 1984 games, but he returned to the games in 1988, at the age of 28, with one goal: to become the first man to win the springboard and platform events at two consecutive Olympiads. (Patricia McCormick, of the United States, did it in 1952 and 1956.) In Seoul, while performing a reverse somersault dive in the preliminary round of the springboard competition, Louganis hit his head on the board. Able to climb out of the pool unassisted, he received four temporary sutures and was back on the board 35 minutes later, earning the highest score by a diver in the preliminaries. The following day, he nailed all 11 of his dives to win his third gold medal.

A week later, Louganis trailed 14-year-old Xiong Ni of China by three points going into the final dive for the platform title. Both performances were nearly perfect, but Louganis's dive had a higher degree of difficulty. He won the gold medal by a mere 1.14 points and reached his goal.

After retiring from competition, the former Olympic athlete became a stage actor and performed in two off-Broadway shows in New York City. He currently lives in Southern California, where he spends much of his time speaking to youth groups about drugs and alcohol and working to help people with dyslexia. Regarding his athletic accomplishments, Louganis said, "I don't want to be remembered as the greatest diver who ever lived. I want to be able to see the greatest diver. I hope to live to see the day when my records are broken." In fact, Louganis did see one of his records broken in 2000. Liang Tian received 724.53 points in the platform competition in Sydney—13.62 points higher than Louganis's 1984 score.

Paavo Nurmi
middle-distance runner

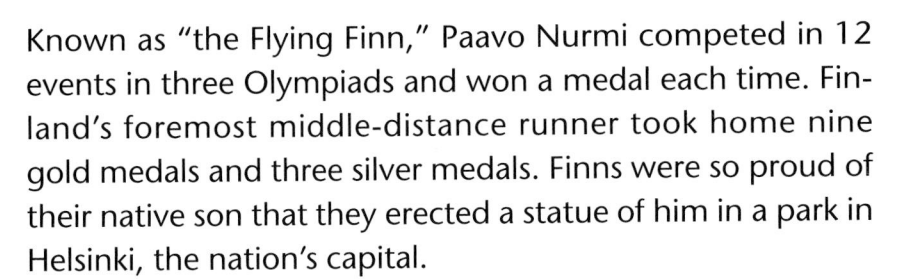

Known as "the Flying Finn," Paavo Nurmi competed in 12 events in three Olympiads and won a medal each time. Finland's foremost middle-distance runner took home nine gold medals and three silver medals. Finns were so proud of their native son that they erected a statue of him in a park in Helsinki, the nation's capital.

Nurmi was born in 1897 to a poor family in Turku, the former Finnish capital. His father, a carpenter, died when Nurmi was only 12 years old. The young boy had to quit school and work so that his family would have enough money to survive. Nurmi got a job running errands, pushing a heavy wheelbarrow through the city streets. As a teenager, Nurmi began running alone through the pine forests near his home. Then, in 1919, while serving in the Finnish army, he took part in a marching race. The soldiers wore heavy boots and carried their rifles. Nurmi was the only soldier who ran the entire distance. Running eventually transformed the quiet young boy into an Olympic champion.

During his career, he set 29 world records at distances from 1,500 meters to 20 kilometers. At the Olympics in

Paavo Nurmi crosses the finish line of the 5,000-meter race at the 1924 Olympics in Paris, winning his second gold medal of the day. Less than an hour earlier, he took the gold in the 1,500-meter event.

FINAL LAP

After retiring from competitive running, Paavo Nurmi made one last appearance on the Olympic track. When the games came to Helsinki in 1952, Nurmi had the honor of carrying the Olympic flame into the stadium. His appearance was a surprise. As he ran the final lap around the stadium track, the crowd remained silent until spectators recognized him. Cheers and applause erupted, and athletes rushed to the edge of the track to catch a glimpse of the legendary Olympian. True to form, Nurmi neither smiled nor waved to his adoring fans. Although he had won 20 national titles for Finland, Nurmi maintained that he trained for personal satisfaction. "I ran for myself, never for Finland," he once said.

1924, Nurmi won gold medals in the 1,500 m, the 5,000 m, the individual cross-country, team cross-country, and the 3,000-m team race.

Nurmi's victories in the 1,500 m and the 5,000 m took amazing stamina and determination. The schedule called for the 5,000-m race to start less than an hour after the 1,500-m race ended. It seemed impossible for a runner to finish one race and to have enough time to rest before the next one—but Nurmi was no ordinary runner. Three weeks before the two Olympic finals, he did a test run. He ran a 1,500-m race in record time (3:52.6). Then, after resting for an hour, Nurmi ran a 5,000-m race, setting another world record (14:28.2).

When the real test came at the 1924 games in Paris, the Flying Finn was ready. For the 1,500-m event, Nurmi decided to set off quickly so he would not have to sprint to the finish with his opponents. The plan worked. He was so far ahead of the others that even though he coasted the final 300 m, he still won by about 10 m. Nurmi's opponents in the 5,000-m event assumed he would be tired from the earlier event, so they set a fast pace at the start of the race in an attempt to lose him. Nurmi took the lead at about the half-way mark of the race. Only his teammate, Ville Ritola, kept up with him. The two Finns battled for the lead. In the final eight laps, with about 60 m remaining, Ritola tried to pass his teammate. Nurmi picked up the pace and never looked back. Checking his stopwatch one last time, Nurmi tossed it to the ground and sprinted to a two-yard victory.

In 1928, Nurmi earned his ninth and final Olympic gold medal, in the 10,000 m—the same event in which he had won his first gold medal in 1920. He again defeated his teammate Ville Ritola by a narrow margin of just a few strides. After crossing the finish line, Nurmi ignored the cheers of the crowd and the congratulations of the other runners, refused to be photographed, gathered up his gear, and quickly disappeared from the stadium. The following week he captured silver medals in the 5,000 m and the steeplechase. The most celebrated distance runner of his time, Nurmi never seemed to enjoy the attention that he certainly deserved. When Nurmi died in 1973 at the age of 76, six Finnish gold medalists came to his funeral to carry the coffin.

Al Oerter
discus thrower

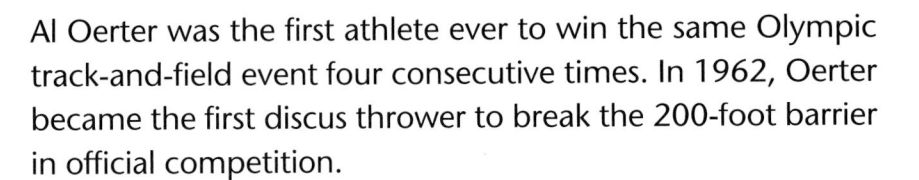

Al Oerter was the first athlete ever to win the same Olympic track-and-field event four consecutive times. In 1962, Oerter became the first discus thrower to break the 200-foot barrier in official competition.

In 1951, when Oerter was growing up in West Babylon, New York, a discus landed on the high school track where he had been running. Oerter, then 15, threw the discus back in the direction from which it had come. Noticing that he had thrown the discus farther than the original throw, the track coach suggested that Oerter consider switching events. He took the coach's suggestion and soon set a national record for high school discus, earning a scholarship to the University of Kansas. Following his sophomore year, Oerter tried out and qualified for the U.S. Olympic team.

With his amazing skill at discus throwing, Al Oerter captured the gold medal in four consecutive Olympiads, setting an Olympic record each time.

TRUE OLYMPIC SPIRIT

Al Oerter is the only athlete to have won gold medals in four consecutive Olympiads. Frank Dolson, a reporter for the *Philadelphia Inquirer*, believed Oerter's accomplishment was the greatest athletic achievement of the century: "It was not the most highly publicized. And certainly not the most highly rewarded in monetary terms. But to an athlete who epitomizes the amateur spirit, [it was] surely the most satisfying."

At the 1956 games in Melbourne, Australia, Oerter made the best throw of his career—184 ft, 11 inches (56.36 m). He beat teammate Fortune Gordien, the world record holder, and won his first gold medal. No one else came within 5 ft of Oerter's winning throw.

Injured in a car collision the following year, Oerter recovered fully and was back in shape for the 1960 games. As defending champion, he was feeling the pressure. "In Rome in 1960 the nervous tension was so bad it was like physical pain," he said. Teammate Rink Babka led off with a toss of 190 ft, 4 inches (58.02 m). Oerter followed with 189 ft, 1 inch (57.63 m), but he could not improve his distance over the next three rounds. As Oerter prepared for his fifth and final throw, Babka recommended that he hold his left arm higher as he spun. Oerter made the adjustment and threw his discus 194 ft, 2 inches (59.18 m), winning his second gold medal.

Oerter's most stunning Olympic performance came in 1964. He knew it would be tough to win a third gold medal. The world record holder at the time, Ludvik Danek of Czechoslovakia, had 45 consecutive wins to his name. Oerter, on the other hand, had torn some rib cartilage a week before the games. Doctors had advised him to rest for several weeks, but he decided to compete anyway. Before the competition, he told another athlete, "If I don't do it on the first throw, I won't be able to do it at all." His first throw only went 189 ft, 1 inch (57.63 m). After four rounds, Oerter was in third place. On his final throw, he gave his all. While he doubled over in agony, his discus sailed 200 ft, 1 inch (61 m) to set another Olympic record and to earn Oerter a third gold medal.

Oerter was performing poorly in the high altitude of Mexico City in 1968. After three rounds, he was in fourth place. Then, as if by magic, Oerter uncorked a record-breaking throw of 212 ft, 6 inches (64.78 m)—5 ft farther than he had ever thrown before. The other competitors, the judges, and the spectators were amazed and astonished. Oerter had won his fourth straight Olympic title for the discus throw. Not once during his Olympic career had he been favored to win. Yet each time he won the gold and set an Olympic record.

Al Oerter retired from competition in 1969 to become a systems analyst and computer engineer. "I think the best thing for me to do is to slide out of this gracefully," he said.

Jesse Owens
sprinter and long jumper

More than four decades after American Jesse Owens retired from track-and-field competition, he is still acknowledged as one of the greatest sprinters ever. At the 1936 games in Berlin, Owens captured four gold medals in the sprints and the long jump and became the first track-and-field athlete to win that many top honors at a single Olympiad. Owens's astonishing performance also struck a powerful blow against racism.

James Cleveland "J.C." Owens was born on September 12, 1913, in Decatur, Alabama. The grandson of slaves and the son of sharecroppers, J.C. worked in the cotton fields when he was a young boy. When he was nine years old, the family moved to Cleveland, Ohio. On the first day at his new school, the teacher asked for his name. When he said "J.C." in his southern drawl, the teacher heard "Jesse," and the name stuck. Owens delivered groceries and worked at a gas station after school to earn money for his family. Track coach Charlie Riley observed Owens's natural talent during gym class. Because Owens had to work after school, Riley agreed to train him in the mornings.

By the time he graduated from high school, Owens had set national records in the long jump and sprints. An athletic scholarship enabled Owens to attend Ohio State University. In one spectacular afternoon during his sophomore year, Owens set three world records and equaled a fourth in less than an hour! This series of amazing feats began when he matched the world record for the 100-yard dash (9.4 seconds). Ten minutes later, Owens set a new world record for the long jump (more than half a foot better than the previous record) that stood for 20 years.

The following year, in 1936, Owens became a legend. Chosen to compete for the United States in the Berlin Olympics, Owens faced more than grueling athletic contests. At the time, Adolf Hitler and the Nazi Party controlled the German government. Eager to prove the superiority of the white race,

Jesse Owens takes off from the starting line, making history as winner of the 100-meter dash and the long jump competitions at the 1936 games in Berlin.

RETURN TO THE GLORY DAYS

In 1950, sportswriters selected Jesse Owens as the greatest track athlete of the half-century. The following year, Owens returned to Berlin for the first time since his Olympic triumph there. During a track meet there, Owens donned his old Olympic suit and jogged around the track to the cheers and applause of 75,000 German spectators.

Hitler ridiculed the United States for allowing African Americans to represent the nation in international competition. As Owens competed in a total of 12 preliminary heats and events, his gold medals piled up—100-meter and 200-m sprints, the long jump, and the 400-m team relay. According to legend, Hitler refused to shake Owens's hand after his stunning victories, but the German leader had actually stopped the public displays of congratulations to the winners prior to Owens's events. Perhaps Hitler anticipated the humiliation of having his pronouncements of superiority disproved.

Owens retired from amateur athletics after the Olympic Games, when he was only 23 years old. Despite his fame and popularity, Owens found it difficult to earn a living. He had his own basketball team for a while and earned some money giving speeches during the presidential campaign of Alf Landon, then governor of Kansas, who was running against Franklin D. Roosevelt. Then, at the end of 1936, Owens received an offer of $2,000 to race against a horse. He accepted the challenge even though many people said it was degrading for an Olympic champion to run against a horse. Owens replied, " . . . but what was I supposed to do? I had four gold medals, but you can't eat four gold medals. There was no television, no big advertising, no endorsements then. Not for a black man, anyway. Things were different then." Owens's energy and optimism helped him survive the bad years. He enjoyed some prosperity as a public speaker during the latter half of his life. Once described as a "professional good example," Owens traveled widely, delivering motivational speeches to community groups, church organizations, and college commencement ceremonies. He also served as Ambassador of Sports for the U.S. State Department. In this position, he traveled to India, Malaysia, Singapore, and the Philippines to meet with government officials, athletic organizations, and youth groups.

In 1976, President Gerald R. Ford awarded Owens with the Medal of Freedom, the highest honor given to a U.S. citizen. Jesse Owens received numerous other awards and honors, many of which were granted after his death from lung cancer in 1980. One such honor came two years later, when a street leading to the Olympic stadium in Berlin was renamed Jesse Owens Allee.

Mary Lou Retton
gymnast

Mary Lou Retton is often credited for helping to transform women's gymnastics from a balletic activity to a sport that requires daring, energy, strength, and amazing agility.

Retton was born in Fairmont, West Virginia, in 1968. She was only eight years old when she watched on television as Nadia Comaneci scored the first perfect ten in Olympic gymnastics, at the 1976 games in Montreal. Inspired by Comaneci's perfect performance, Retton began gymnastics classes with a goal to become an Olympic gymnast. By the time she was 12, Retton was competing with older and more experienced gymnasts. Entered in the 1980 Class 1 Nationals, she won the vault event, came in second in the floor exercise, and finished seventh in the all-around competition. The following year, Retton joined the U.S. Junior National Team and began to compete internationally.

In 1982, at a competition in Las Vegas, Retton met Bela Karolyi, who had coached Nadia Comaneci. Karolyi invited Retton to train at his school in Houston. After only two weeks with her new coach, Retton scored her first perfect ten. Two months later, she defeated America's top female gymnasts at a meet in Las Vegas. She was on her way to Olympic gold.

To prepare for the 1984 games, Retton began a grueling schedule, training 8 to 10 hours a day. She won a place on the U.S. women's team. Just before the Los Angeles games, Retton tore the cartilage in her right knee. Two days after arthroscopic surgery to repair the damage, Retton returned to her hectic training schedule. She led the team to a silver medal in the team competition—the first Olympic gymnastics medal for U.S. women since 1948. Retton went on to execute a perfect Tsukahara (a back somersault with a double twist) to capture the all-around title and to become the first American woman to win an individual medal in gymnastics. She also was the youngest gymnast and most decorated U.S. athlete at the Los Angeles games.

Coach Karolyi said that Retton was the most positive and dedicated student he had ever coached. Retton added, "I work at this seven days a week. And at night I sometimes dream gymnastics."

Knowing she performed well, Mary Lou Retton raises her arms and smiles broadly as she finishes her routine in the floor exercise competition at the 1984 Olympics.

Vitaly Scherbo

gymnast

At the 1992 Summer Olympics in Barcelona, Spain, Vitaly Scherbo won six gold medals in gymnastics—the most by a gymnast at a single Olympiad. Even more astounding, he won four of these—pommel horse, rings, vault, and parallel bars—in a single day!

Scherbo was born in 1972 in Minsk, a city in present-day Belarus. The son of acrobats, he took up gymnastics when he was only 7 years old. It was a time when the Soviet Union placed great emphasis on sports and the training of its athletes. At the age of 15, Scherbo joined the Soviet national team, attending the country's main training school in Moscow. By the age of 20, Scherbo had become one of the greatest male gymnasts of all time. Between 1991 and 1996, he earned 26 medals (including 18 gold) in Olympic and world championship competitions. His six gold medals at the Barcelona games represented one of the greatest Olympic triumphs ever. "Obviously, I'm thrilled," said Scherbo. "I certainly didn't expect this to happen."

The only event in which Scherbo failed to capture a gold was the floor exercise, which some consider his specialty. Scherbo had been penalized one-tenth of a point when he stepped out of bounds on a tumbling run. He finished in sixth place in that event but came back two years later to capture the gold at the 1994 world championships.

When Scherbo was growing up, Belarus was part of the Soviet Union. With the breakup of the Soviet Union in 1991, Belarus became a separate country. Scherbo competed for the Unified Team at the 1992 Olympic Games. During the five individual gold medal ceremonies for Scherbo, the flag of Belarus was raised and its national anthem was played for the first time ever at the Olympic games.

After the Barcelona games, Scherbo returned to Belarus, where life had become difficult for many people. After Scherbo's apartment was broken into and robbed, he and his wife, Irina, moved to Pennsylvania. There they could live in safety while he trained at the Woodward Gymnastic Camp. Although he was living and training in the United States, Scherbo continued to compete for Belarus.

Vitaly Scherbo's skill on the rings earned him first place in both the individual all-around competition and the individual apparatus finals at the 1992 games in Barcelona.

The emotional high of Scherbo's successes was short lived. Several months before the 1996 Olympic Games, Irina was critically injured in an automobile crash. The accident left her in a coma for more than a month. During this time, Scherbo gave up gymnastics to sit by his wife's bedside. Despite little hope for her survival, Irina miraculously emerged from her unconscious state. As she began to recover, Irina insisted that Scherbo resume his training for the upcoming Summer Games in Atlanta. Although 15 pounds overweight, he refocused his goals and began to train in earnest. He hoped to become the first Olympic gymnast to win back-to-back all-around titles since Japan's Sawao Kato had done so in 1968 and 1972. It didn't happen. Scherbo won bronze medals in the all-around, horizontal bar, parallel bars, and vault. Unable to hide his disappointment about not winning gold, he reportedly said, "In my family we don't know of medals of any other color." Among his many awards and honors, Vitaly Scherbo was named the Best Athlete in the World in 1992 by *Trans World Sport*, a popular television show.

Mark Spitz
swimmer

Mark Spitz proudly displays five of his gold medals from the 1972 games. Spitz captured a historic total of seven gold medals at the Munich games in 1972.

The year was 1972, the place was Munich, Germany, and the undisputed star of the show was American swimmer Mark Spitz. He entered seven swimming events, winning an unprecedented seven gold medals while establishing seven world records. He had become the most decorated athlete in any single Olympiad.

California-born Spitz began swimming competitively when he was eight years old. At the University of Indiana, Spitz won eight National Collegiate Athletic Association (NCAA) titles. His best strokes were freestyle and butterfly.

Preparing for the 1968 games in Mexico City, Spitz expected to win six gold medals. The pressure proved to be too much for him, however. He won two gold medals in the relays but only a silver and a bronze in the individual events. In his final event—the 200-meter butterfly, for which he held the world record—Spitz finished a very disappointing last. He called it "the worst meet of my life."

Four years later, Spitz pulled off an amazing turnaround. He took the gold in the 100-meter freestyle (51.22); the 200-m freestyle (1:52.78); the 100-m butterfly (54.27); the 200-m butterfly (2:00.70); the 400-m freestyle relay (3:26.42); the 800-m freestyle relay (7:35.78); and the 400-m medley relay (3:48.16).

Capitalizing on his Olympic fame, Spitz accepted several offers for endorsements. Hoping to make $20,000, enough to pay his way through dental school, he received an estimated $5 million in endorsement contracts in the year following the Munich games. He also posed for what became one of the most popular posters of an athlete ever made—wearing only his red, white, and blue bathing suit and all seven gold medals. Spitz retired from swimming to open a real estate development business with his endorsement earnings. Then, in 1990, he announced that he would make a comeback. The experts called it a long shot, but Spitz was eager for a challenge. Although he trained seriously, he failed to qualify for a spot on the 1992 Olympic swim team in the 100-m butterfly. At age 40, he was simply no match for swimmers half his age.

Teófilo Stevenson
boxer

Teófilo Stevenson was one of the greatest heavyweight boxers ever, even though he never won the world's heavyweight championship. This is because the Cuban government prohibited him from becoming a professional prizefighter. Stevenson was allowed to fight only as an amateur in the Olympics. Competing in three Olympiads, he won every time he entered the ring.

Stevenson's first appearance on the international boxing scene was at the 1971 Pan-American Games. In the semifinals, Stevenson lost a decision to Duane Bobick of the United States. At the 1972 games in Munich, Germany, the two boxers met again. Bobick was confident of another win. "I know [Stevenson is] tall and strong," Bobick said, "but the last time all he had was a good jab—no right hand." What the American did not know was that his Cuban opponent had spent the previous year working to improve the power of his right-hand punch.

In the rematch in Munich, Stevenson continued to use his comfortable left jab, but he also displayed his surprising

Teófilo Stevenson ruled the ring at the 1980 games, winning the gold in the heavyweight category in his third consecutive Olympiad.

new hammerlike right-hand punch to demolish Bobick. The referee stopped the fight in the third round.

Professional boxing promoters longed for the chance to manage the 20-year-old Cuban fighter. Teófilo Stevenson was talented and handsome, and his 6-foot, 3.5-inch frame was solid muscle. Stevenson refused to turn professional, however, even turning down $1 million, because he wished to box solely for the honor of his country.

Over the next four years, Stevenson lost only two fights, both to Igor Vysotsky of the Soviet Union. The Russian boxer was unable to compete at the 1976 games in Montreal because of an eye injury, however. With his main rival out of the competition, another gold medal was easily within the Cuban fighter's grasp. Stevenson downed his first three opponents, beating all of them in a total time of just 7 minutes and 22 seconds. His opponent in the final, Romania's Mircea Simion, was understandably intimidated. Simion managed to avoid the Cuban for almost three full rounds, but he was unable to do that indefinitely. When Stevenson finally hit Simion squarely in the jaw, Simion's cornermen threw a towel into the ring to stop the fight with only 25 seconds left. Stevenson had won his second consecutive gold medal. Again he refused an offer to turn professional. "I will not trade the Cuban people for all the dollars in the world," he said. "What is a million dollars against eight million Cubans who love me?"

Stevenson's third gold medal came at the 1980 games in Moscow. He was so much better than his opponents that it was not until the semifinals that any of his Olympic rivals could survive the full three rounds against him.

In addition to his Olympic medals, Stevenson triumphed at the Pan-American Games in 1975 and 1979 and was world amateur champion in 1974, 1978, and 1986. As late as 1986, at the age of 34, Stevenson won the world amateur championship.

Following his retirement from the ring, Stevenson worked as a boxing adviser for the Cuban national sports institute, where he earned about $400 a month. Did he ever regret passing up millions of dollars by not turning professional? He says no. "There are world champions who earn a lot of money," he said, "but they don't even know how to sign their names. . . . I have what I need. I am happy."

Jim Thorpe
decathlete and pentathlete

One of the greatest athletes ever to compete in the Olympic Games, James Francis Thorpe was the only man in history to win the ten-event decathlon and the five-event pentathlon. Although he was competing in the decathlon for the first time, he set a world record (8,412 points) that stood as an Olympic record for 20 years.

Thorpe was born in 1888 on a farm in Oklahoma to parents who were part Native American. Thorpe's Indian name was Wa-Tho-Huck, which means "Bright Path," but sadness trailed him from an early age. At 10, his twin brother, Charles, died of pneumonia, and by the time he was 15, Thorpe had lost both parents. Thorpe attended the Carlisle Indian School in Pennsylvania, where he excelled at sports. He could do it all. He competed successfully in every sport just for the joy of it. His track coach, Glenn Scobie "Pop" Warner, recognized Thorpe's potential as a football player. In the most important game of the 1911 season, Thorpe scored four field goals and ran 70 yards for a touchdown and a victory against Harvard. The following season, after his Olympic triumphs, he led Carlisle to an upset victory over the mighty Army team. Catching the ball after an Army kickoff, Thorpe ran 95 yards for a touchdown. There was no stopping him that season—he scored 25 touchdowns and a total of 198 points in 14 games.

At the 1912 Olympic Games in Stockholm, Sweden, Thorpe began by winning the gold medal in the pentathlon—a strenuous five-event contest consisting of long jump, javelin throw, 200-meter race, discus throw, and 1,500-m race. Thorpe finished first in four events and placed third in the javelin throw, which is not surprising since he had never thrown a javelin until two months before the Olympics. He then competed in the high jump and the long jump, finishing in fourth and seventh places, respectively. Finally, he participated in the decathlon, easily winning the

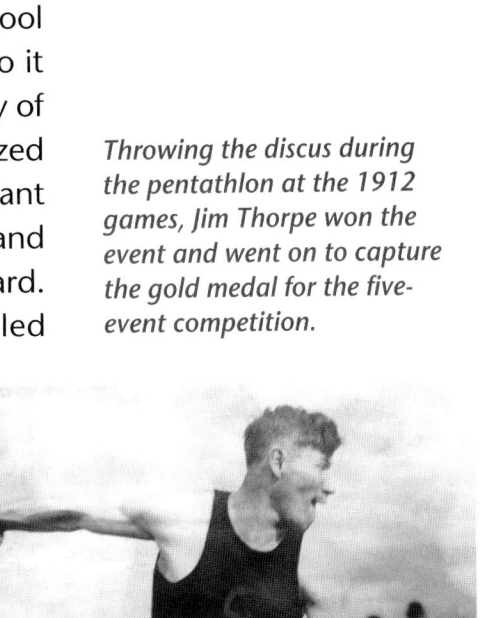

Throwing the discus during the pentathlon at the 1912 games, Jim Thorpe won the event and went on to capture the gold medal for the five-event competition.

A SIMPLE THANK YOU

At the medal ceremony in 1912, Gustav V, King of Sweden, presented Thorpe with a bust of himself and a jewel-encrusted goblet from Tsar Nicholas of Russia. In presenting the gifts to Thorpe, the king remarked "Sir, you are the greatest athlete in the world." The usually shy athlete simply replied, "Thanks, King."

ten events—100-m dash, long jump, shot put, high jump, 400-m race, discus throw, 110-m hurdles, pole vault, javelin throw, and 1,500-m race. Thorpe led a ticker-tape parade in New York City following his victories in Stockholm. A year after the Stockholm Olympiad, the Amateur Athletic Union and IOC officials learned that Thorpe had played minor league baseball in 1909 and 1910. Thorpe was declared a "professional" and stripped of his gold medals. It was a crushing blow because he had not played for the money (which had been about $2 a game) but because "[he] liked to play ball."

Jim Thorpe returned his medals, which were subsequently awarded to Ferdinand Bie (Norway) and Hugo Wieslander (Sweden), who had come in second in the pentathlon and decathlon, respectively. Wieslander refused to even open the box containing the medal. He sent it back to the Olympic Committee with a note saying, "I didn't win the Olympic championship. James Thorpe won it. I do not know what your rules are in regard to amateurism in America, but I do know that Thorpe is the greatest athlete in the world."

After his initial disappointment, Thorpe received offers to play major league baseball. He signed with the New York Giants for a time and later played for the Cincinnati Reds and the Boston Braves. From 1915 to 1928, he also played professional football for the Canton Bulldogs, Cleveland Rams, New York Giants, and the Chicago Cardinals. In 1920, the American Professional Football Association (which later became the National Football League) was formed. Thorpe became its first president.

In 1951, Hollywood released *Jim Thorpe—All American,* a movie based on the athlete's life. Thorpe died in poverty in 1953, three years after Associated Press sportswriters voted him the greatest athlete of the first half of the 20th century. A decade later, he became the first player elected into the Football Hall of Fame. Visitors to the hall will see a seven-foot statue of him—bigger than life, just like the man. Efforts to reinstate Thorpe's Olympic records and trophies continued for decades. Even President Gerald Ford wrote a letter to the IOC on Thorpe's behalf. In 1982, the IOC finally lifted the ban, allowed his name to be returned to the record books as "co-champion" of the decathlon and pentathlon, and presented his children with replicas of the medals he had won.

Emil Zátopek
distance runner

At the 1952 Olympic Games in Helsinki, Finland, Emil Zátopek of Czechoslovakia won the 5,000-meter and 10,000-m runs, and the marathon. No athlete before—or since—has won those three races at a single Olympiad. Even more amazing, the marathon was the first Zátopek had ever run. During his career, Zátopek won a spectacular 261 of 334 races (of all lengths and distances) and set 18 world records.

Zátopek did not look like a world-class athlete when he ran. His face was bright red, his head rolled from side to side, and he groaned and gasped. But Zátopek was not concerned with his appearance, "I was interested in my finish, not in being beautiful."

Born in 1922 in Moravia, Czechoslovakia, to a carpenter and his wife, Zátopek was the seventh of eight children. He left home at 16, took a job in a shoe factory, and began running. When he was 18, his manager at the factory encouraged him to participate in a race throughout the city. He did not want to run and tried to get out of the race by saying he had a cold and a bad knee. The manager insisted that Zátopek see the company doctor, who reported that he was in perfect health. Zátopek ran that day and surprised himself by coming in in second place.

Emil Zátopek leads the pack around the final turn to win the gold in the 5,000-meter race during the 1952 games in Helsinki.

ALL IN THE FAMILY

Both Emil Zátopek and his wife, Dana, won gold medals at the 1952 Olympics. After winning his first gold medal first, he showed it to his wife. She put it in her equipment bag "for luck" and went to the javelin competition area. On her first throw, she set an Olympic record and earned a gold medal of her own. He would, of course, win two more at that Olympiad. The gold medal leaders in track and field at the 1952 games were the United States with 15 and the Zátopeks with 4.

After he was drafted into the army, Zátopek invented new ways to train. For example, he would run around the track to near exhaustion wearing heavy combat boots. To increase his lung capacity, he ran as far as he could while holding his breath. He developed interval training, a technique that most competitive runners now use. Instead of running the entire 10,000-m distance while training for that event, he might run five repetitions of 200 m, then 20 repetitions of 400 m, then five more repetitions of 200 m, all at top speed, with a light jog of about a minute between each repetition.

At the 1948 games in London, Zátopek won the silver medal in the 5,000-m race and the gold medal in the 10,000-m competition. In the latter contest, Zátopek outran the field to cross the finish line about 300 m (328 feet) before the second-place runner.

At the 1952 games in Helsinki, Zátopek became the first runner in 40 years to win the gold in both the 5,000-m and 10,000-m events at the same Olympiad, setting new Olympic records in both races. Not satisfied with those achievements, he entered the marathon, as well. Although he had never before run a marathon, Zátopek seemed unconcerned. At about the ten-mile mark, Zátopek found himself running alongside Jim Peters of Great Britain, the favored runner. He took the opportunity to ask Peters if his pace was too fast. The Englishman replied jokingly, "Emil, the pace—it is too slow." That was all Zátopek needed to hear; he simply took off. A few miles later, the British runner quit and Zátopek increased his lead. As he entered the stadium for the final lap, the huge crowd greeted him by chanting his name, "Zátopek! Zátopek! Zátopek!" He had finished the race two minutes ahead of the next runner, setting yet another Olympic record.

Despite recovering from surgery to repair a hernia, Zátopek returned to the Olympics in 1956 to run one more marathon. Although his doctors advised against it, he resumed training shortly after leaving the hospital. Amazingly, he finished sixth in Melbourne, retiring as an Olympic champion and competitive runner in 1958. Although controversy arose when he spoke against the Soviet Union's 1968 takeover of Czechoslovakia, Zátopek remained popular for his athletic achievements and his sportsmanship. Emil Zátopek died in 2000 at the age of 78.

THE SUMMER GAMES

Year	City, Nation
1896	Athens, Greece
1900	Paris, France
1904	St. Louis, Missouri, USA
1908	London, England
1912	Stockholm, Sweden
1916	canceled
1920	Antwerp, Belgium
1924	Paris, France
1928	Amsterdam, Holland
1932	Los Angeles, California, USA
1936	Berlin, Germany
1940	canceled
1944	canceled
1948	London, England
1952	Helsinki, Finland
1956	Melbourne, Australia
1960	Rome, Italy
1964	Tokyo, Japan
1968	Mexico City, Mexico
1972	Munich, Germany
1976	Montreal, Canada
1980	Moscow, USSR
1984	Los Angeles, California, USA
1988	Seoul, South Korea
1992	Barcelona, Spain
1996	Atlanta, Georgia, USA
2000	Sydney, Australia
2004	Athens, Greece

GOLD MEDAL TIMES

Listed below are the gold medal winners in selected events.

* **Olympic Record**
** **World Record**
*** **World Best** (Because the marathon course varies in each host city, the fastest times are considered to be "World Bests," and not World Records.)

Track and Field

MEN: marathon

Year	Winner	Time
1896	Spyridon Louis, Greece	2:58:50
1900	Michel Théato, France	2:59:45
1904	Thomas Hicks, USA	3:28:53
1908	John Hayes, USA	2:55:18.4*
1912	Kenneth McArthur, South Africa	2:36:54.8
1920	Hannes Kolehmainen, Finland	2:32:35.8***
1924	Albin Stenroos, Finland	2:41:22.6
1928	Boughera El Ouafi, France	2:32:57
1932	Juan Carlos Zabala, Argentina	2:31:36*
1936	Sohn Kee-Chung, Japan (Korea)	2:29:19.2*
1948	Delfo Cabrera, Argentina	2:34:51.6
1952	Emil Zátopek, Czechoslovakia	2:23:03.2*
1956	Alain Mimoun, France	2:25:00
1960	Abebe Bikila, Ethiopia	2:15:16.2***
1964	Abebe Bikila, Ethiopia	2:12:11.2***
1968	Mamo Wolde, Ethiopia	2:20:26.4
1972	Frank Shorter, USA	2:12:19.8
1976	Waldemar Cierpinski, East Germany	2:09:55*
1980	Waldemar Cierpinski, East Germany	2:11:03
1984	Carlos Lopes, Portugal	2:09:21*
1988	Gelindo Bordin, Italy	2:10:32
1992	Hwang Young-Cho, South Korea	2:13:23
1996	Josia Thugwane, South Africa	2:12:36
2000	Gezahgne Abera, Ethiopia	2:10:11

long jump

1896	Ellery Clark, USA	20'10"
1900	Alvin Kraenzlein, USA	23'6¾"*
1904	Meyer Prinstein, USA	24'1"*
1908	Francis "Frank" Irons, USA	24'6½"*
1912	Albert Gutterson, USA	24'11¼"*
1920	William Petersson, Sweden	23'5½"
1924	William DeHart Hubbard, USA	24'5"
1928	Edward B. Hamm, USA	25'4½"*
1932	Edward Gordon, USA	25'¾"
1936	Jesse Owens, USA	26'5½"*
1948	William Steele, USA	25'8"
1952	Jerome Biffle, USA	24'10"
1956	Gregory Bell, USA	25'8¼"
1960	Ralph Boston, USA	26'7¾"*
1964	Lynn Davies, Great Britain	26'5¾"
1968	Bob Beamon, USA	29'2½"**
1972	Randy Williams, USA	27'½"
1976	Clarence "Arnie" Robinson, USA	27'4¼"
1980	Lutz Dombrowski, East Germany	28'¼"
1984	Carl Lewis, USA	28'¼"
1988	Carl Lewis, USA	28'7½"
1992	Carl Lewis, USA	28'5½"
1996	Carl Lewis, USA	27'10¼"
2000	Ivan Pedroso, Cuba	28'¾"

discus throw

1896	Robert Garrett, USA	95'7½"
1900	Rudolf Bauer, Hungary	118'3"*
1904	Martin Sheridan, USA	128'10½"*
1908	Martin Sheridan, USA	134'2"*
1912	Armas Taipale, Finland	148'3"*
1920	Elmer Niklander, Finland	146'7"
1924	Clarence "Bud" Houser, USA	151'4"*
1928	Clarence "Bud" Houser, USA	155'3"*
1932	John Anderson, USA	162'4"*
1936	Ken Carpenter, USA	165'7"*
1948	Adolfo Consolini, Italy	173'2"*
1952	Sim Iness, USA	180'6"*
1956	Al Oerter, USA	184'11"*
1960	Al Oerter, USA	194'2"*

1964	Al Oerter, USA	200′1″*
1968	Al Oerter, USA	212′6″*
1972	Ludvik Danek, Czechoslovakia	211′3″
1976	Maurice "Mac" Wilkins, USA	221′5″
1980	Viktor Rashchupkin, USSR	218′8″
1984	Rolf Dannenberg, West Germany	218′6″
1988	Jürgen Schult, East Germany	225′9″*
1992	Romas Ubartas, Lithuania	213′8″
1996	Lars Riedel, Germany	227′8″*
2000	Virgilijus Alekna, Lithuania	227′4″

WOMEN: javelin throw

1932	Mildred "Babe" Didrikson, USA	143′4″*
1936	Tilly Fleischer, Germany	148′3″*
1948	Hermine "Herma" Bauma, Austria	149′6″*
1952	Dana Zátopková, Czechoslovakia	165′7″*
1956	Inese Jaunzeme, USSR	176′8″*
1960	Elvira Ozolina, USSR	183′8″*
1964	Mihaela Penes, Romania	198′7″
1968	Angéla Németh, Hungary	198′0″
1972	Ruth Fuchs, East Germany	209′7″*
1976	Ruth Fuchs, East Germany	216′4″*
1980	María Colón Rueñes, Cuba	224′5″*
1984	Tessa Sanderson, Great Britain	228′2″*
1988	Petra Felke, East Germany	245′0″*
1992	Silke Renk, Germany	224′2″
1996	Heli Rantanen, Finland	222′11″
2000	Trine Hattestad, Norway	226′1½″*

Swimming

MEN: 100-meter freestyle

1896	Alfréd Hajós, Hungary	1:22.2*
1904	Zoltán Halmaj, Hungary (100 yards)	1:02.8
1908	Charles Daniels, USA	1:05.6**
1912	Duke Kahanamoku, USA	1:03.4
1920	Duke Kahanamoku, USA	1:00.4**
1924	P. "Johnny" Weissmuller, USA	59.0*
1928	P. "Johnny" Weissmuller, USA	58.6*
1932	Yasuji Miyazaki, Japan	58.2

1936	Ferenc Csík, Hungary	57.6
1948	Wally Ris, USA	57.3*
1952	Clarke Scholes, USA	57.4
1956	John Henricks, Australia	55.4*
1960	John Devitt, Australia	55.2*
1964	Don Schollander, USA	53.4*
1968	Mike Wenden, Australia	52.2**
1972	Mark Spitz, USA	51.22**
1976	Jim Montgomery, USA	49.99**
1980	Jörg Woithe, East Germany	50.4
1984	Ambrose "Rowdy" Gaines, USA	49.8*
1988	Matt Biondi, USA	48.63*
1992	Aleksandr Popov, Unified Team	49.02
1996	Aleksandr Popov, Russia	48.74
2000	Pieter Hoogenband, Netherlands	48.30

WOMEN: 100-meter freestyle

1912	Sarah "Fanny" Durack, Australia	1:22.2
1920	Ethelda Bleibtrey, USA	1:13.6**
1924	Ethel Lackie, USA	1:12.4
1928	Albina Osipowich, USA	1:11.0*
1932	Helene Madison, USA	1:06.8*
1936	Hendrika Mastenbroek, Netherlands	1:05.9*
1948	Greta Andersen, Denmark	1:06.3
1952	Katalin Szöke, Hungary	1:06.8
1956	Dawn Fraser, Australia	1:02.0**
1960	Dawn Fraser, Australia	1:01.2*
1964	Dawn Fraser, Australia	59.5*
1968	Jan Henne, USA	1:00.0
1972	Sandra Neilson, USA	58.59*
1976	Kornelia Ender, East Germany	55.65**
1980	Barbara Krause, East Germany	54.79**
1984	Carrie Steinseifer, USA	55.92
	Nancy Hogshead, USA (tie)	
1988	Kristin Otto, East Germany	54.93
1992	Zhuang Yong, China	54.64*
1996	Le Jingyi, China	54.5*
2000	Inge de Bruijn, Netherlands	53.83

SUGGESTED BOOKS

Anderson, Dave. *The Story of the Olympics.* New York: William Morrow and Company, 1996.

*Ballheimer, David, and Chris Oxlade. *Olympics.* (Eyewitness Series.) New York: Dorling Kindersley, 2000.

Chronicle of the Olympics. New York: Dorling Kindersley, 1998.

Conners, Martin, et al., eds. *The Olympic Factbook: A Spectator's Guide to the Summer Games.* Detroit: Visible Ink Press, 1992.

*Costain, Meredith. *Olympic Summer Games 2000.* New York: Penguin Putnam Books, 2000.

*Italia, Robert. *100 Unforgettable Moments in the Summer Olympics.* Minneapolis: ABDO Publishing Company, 1998.

Johnson, William Oscar. *The Olympics: A History of the Games.* New York: Bishop Books, Inc., 1996.

*Knotts, Bob. *The Summer Olympics.* Danbury, CT.: Children's Press, 2000.

Kristy, Davida. *Coubertin's Olympics: How the Games Began.* Minneapolis: Lerner Publishing Group, 1995.

Leder, Jane. *Grace & Glory: A Century of Women in the Olympics.* Chicago: Triumph Books, 1996.

Levinson, David, and Karen Christensen, eds. *Encyclopedia of World Sport.* Denver: ABC-CLIO, 1996.

Mallon, Bill. *Total Olympics: The Complete Record of Every Event in Every Olympics.* New York: Total Sports Publishing, Inc., 2000.

Pursuit of Excellence: The Olympic Story. Danbury, CT.: Grolier Enterprises, Inc., 1979.

Wallechinsky, David. *The Complete Book of the Summer Olympics.* New York: Overlook Press, 2000.

Woff, Richard. *The Ancient Greek Olympics.* New York: Oxford University Press, 2000.

* Denotes book for younger readers

INDEX

Page numbers in *italics* indicate photographs.

PHOTO CREDITS